I0811079

IMAGES
of America

William S. Hart Park

HART PARK FUN MAP. This is the Friends of Hart Park (FOHP) Fun Map created by artist and FOHP director Tim Murphy. Inspired by classic Disneyland maps, Murphy created this cheerful map of the grounds of William S. Hart Park in downtown Newhall, California, during the COVID-19 lockdown in 2020. (Courtesy of Tim Murphy.)

ON THE COVER: William S. Hart stands next to the ranch house on Horseshoe Ranch (today's William S. Hart Park) in Newhall in this undated photograph. Hart retired to the ranch after completing a phenomenally successful 11-year career in silent films. (Courtesy of Roger and Becki Basham.)

IMAGES
of America

WILLIAM S. HART PARK

Bill West, E.J. Stephens,
and Kim Stephens
Foreword by Laurene Weste

ARCADIA
PUBLISHING

ISBN 978-1-4671-0744-0

Published by Arcadia Publishing
Charleston, South Carolina

Printed in the United States of America

Library of Congress Control Number: 2021951884

For all general information, please contact Arcadia Publishing:
Telephone 843-853-2070
Fax 843-853-0044
E-mail sales@arcadiapublishing.com
For customer service and orders:
Toll-Free 1-888-313-2665

Visit us on the Internet at www.arcadiapublishing.com

Dedicated to the generosity of William S. Hart, who gifted his home and ranch to his many fans who gave him their nickels, dimes, and quarters throughout his film career. And to the many employees and volunteers of Hart Park who have invested thousands of hours of sweat equity over the years maintaining his legacy.

CONTENTS

ACKNOWLEDGMENTS

The authors would like to thank the staff and volunteers of William S. Hart Park, the Los Angeles County Department of Parks and Recreation, and the Natural History Museum of Los Angeles County (NHM) for their assistance in this project, and for their ongoing efforts to maintain and enhance this very special place. Special thanks go to Hart Park Museum administrator Magdalyne Romero, County of Los Angeles park superintendent Eric Reifman, and the park's dedicated animal keeper Rachael Komulainen, without all of whom this book would not have been possible.

They would also like to thank the FOHP board of directors: Janis Ashley, Becki Basham, Tim Burkhart, Gladys Farrell, Nancy Gallardo, Tom Hough, Sheila Miller, Tim Murphy, Patti Rasmussen, Michelle Rennie, Jack Stewart, Candy Veluzat, Laurene Weste, Jeff Wheat, and Leon Worden. The same goes for the board of directors of the Santa Clarita Valley Historical Society (SCVHS): Sarah Brewer, Dianne Hellrigel, Guy Horanberg, Pat Horanberg, Tom Hough, Cathy Martin, Barbara Martinelli, Meredith McGowan, Dr. Alan Pollack, Philip Scorza, Ann Stansell, Laurene Weste, Greg Wilzbach, Leon Worden, and Sue Yurosek.

A very special thank-you goes to Roger and Becki Basham, two super-volunteers who provided many of the images and information found in this book. If not for their continued devotion to this project, this book would have never seen the light of day.

Thanks also to Leon Worden, the president of SCVTV and scvhistory.com, and board member of both the SCVHS and FOHP, for many of the images and related information. And thank you to Santa Clarita city council member and FOHP president Laurene Weste for her encouragement and for the foreword to the book.

Bill West wishes to thank his co-authors Kim and E.J. Despite his name being listed first on this book, in truth, Kim is the brains behind the operation, and E.J. is its soul. Bill also thanks his Hart DVD collecting pen-pals Bill and Zettia Miller, who led him down the path to learning and appreciating William S. Hart's film history. Finally, Bill's efforts would not have been possible without the love, support, and patience of his wife and son, Liliana and Josh West.

E.J. and Kimi wish to thank Mariah and Dylan, our coauthor Bill West, and all the great folks in Santa Clarita who continually strive to make this city one of the best places to live in America.

All images are courtesy of scvhistory.com unless otherwise noted.

FOREWORD

When you step into William S. Hart Park, you enter a very special place where the Old West meets the golden age of the silent film era. The brilliant magician who wove these two worlds together was nickelodeon cowboy hero William Surrey Hart. Born in 1864, Hart experienced the Old West firsthand as a youngster and was dedicated to bringing its authentic look to his audiences in his 70-plus films.

Hart brought his love of the American West to Horseshoe Ranch, his retirement home in Newhall, California. His mansion on the hill, La Loma de Los Vientos, displays famous Western paintings by Frederic Remington and Charles Russell. And his great appreciation for America's earliest inhabitants is evident throughout with several pieces of Native American art and artifacts on display.

Hart left his ranch to the people of Los Angeles County in his will, and in September 1958, Hart Park was dedicated for the benefit of the American public of every race and creed. Since then, an enormous number of events have taken place on its 265 acres. In Hart Hall, there have been quilt and rose shows, train exhibits, and dances too numerous to count. Every August, Silents Under the Stars honors Hart's film career with a showing of one of his movies outdoors, under the stars. Cowboys & Carols has been a fan favorite for years during the holidays when the mansion gets beautifully decorated for the season. Lina Schultz and former Hart Park superintendent Norm Phillips have proudly produced the Hart of the West Pow Wow for over 20 years. The Animal Fair has taught thousands of children about barnyard, exotic, and endangered animal species. In the past decade, the City of Santa Clarita has moved its famous Cowboy Festival to Hart Park, and in 2020, E.J. Stephens and Phil Lantis created the Newhallywood Silent Film Festival. And since he was such a great animal lover, I imagine Bill would have especially loved the annual Bow Wows & Meows pet adoptions for shelter animals.

I have been blessed to have been at so many of these gatherings. I also remember attending picnics in the park with the world-famous Cliffie Stone Band. Once, I even got to ride a camel in Hart Park!

I've also seen a devastating fire sweep through the park in the 1970s, the pole barn that later became Hart Hall used by FEMA as the 1994 earthquake relief headquarters, and several historic structures moved here to be saved and restored by the Santa Clarita Valley Historical Society. I was also around for the birth of the Friends of Hart Park in 1985, an organization dedicated to the preservation of Hart's legacy. I am proud of the work they have done over the years raising funds to support the care of the park's animals and to enhance the park's guest experience.

Since 1958, Hart Park has experienced endless change in an attempt to improve for this and future generations. What's next? Who knows, but there are countless ways to honor Hart's legacy in the future, just as his life has influenced the world for over a century now. Hart's generous gift is one that truly keeps on giving.

Thank you, Bill!

Laurene Weste
President, Friends of Hart Park

INTRODUCTION

If we could be magically transported back to Southern California's Santa Clarita Valley during the second decade of the 20th century, we would not find the present-day city of Santa Clarita teeming with its quarter-million inhabitants. Instead, we would encounter the villages of Newhall and Saugus, separated by miles of open range, with only a few hundred residents in both towns.

One of the early inhabitants of Newhall was known to millions of film fans around the world as "Two-Gun Bill," a silent Western hero who let his fists and six-shooters do the talking, and in the process, created the prototypical lone, stoic, strong, silent Western star the world would later see emulated by everyone from Gary Cooper to Clint Eastwood. Two-Gun Bill was the character created by William S. Hart, who earned millions entertaining the world in over 70 enormously popular shoot 'em ups, famous for their action and authenticity.

Newhall and Saugus, now districts of Santa Clarita, looked much different when Bill Hart lived in the area. These communities were surrounded by miles of open chaparral-covered hills in a valley enclosed by the Santa Susana and San Gabriel Mountains. The region was just a few years removed from the era of the Old West, and in many ways still was the Old West. The valley witnessed examples of every tale associated with that colorful era of Western American history, including cattle drives, oil wildcatters, range wars, gold prospectors, water disputes, gunfights, stagecoaches, railroaders, land speculators, Native Americans, fires, floods, and feuds. This was the land of the cowboy, with the horse the main mode of transportation.

A few years after the close of the frontier, the valley saw another fascinating group of newcomers. These recent arrivals came to reenact these earlier events, but this time with the hope of entertaining a worldwide audience. They came from Hollywood, only 25 miles to the south yet a world away. While the city of Hollywood was renowned for its glamour, Newhall was primarily the domain of cattle, which vastly outnumbered its human residents. Occasionally, some of the moviemakers would take a liking to the valley and decide to stay. This was true of Harry Carey, John Wayne's idol, who lived for many years on a ranch in Saugus. Hoot Gibson, another nickelodeon Western star, spent some time here as well hosting a rodeo in town. But by far the most famous filmmaker to make Newhall his home was Hart.

Like many Western stars, Hart was not from the West. He was born in 1864 in Newburgh, New York. But unlike most of the others, he spent many of his formative years in the West, traveling with his itinerant mill worker father. At the age of 15, Hart was living with his family in New York City where, while working as a messenger boy, he got his first taste of show business when given theater passes as payment for his delivery services. It was not long before he was bitten by the acting bug. To learn the craft, he traveled to England, working his way across the Atlantic on a cattle boat. In 1887, at the age of 23, Hart made his stage debut in a production of Shakespeare's *Romeo and Juliet*. More roles soon followed in productions of *Ben Hur, The Virginian, The Squaw Man*, and *The Trail of the Lonesome Pine*. Hart's lanky, 180-pound, six-foot-two-inch frame, piercing blue eyes, and finely chiseled features allowed him to be cast as both hero and villain. For the next several years, he made his living on the stage, both in New York and throughout the country in traveling troupes. As he writes in his autobiography, "I was considered the outstanding portrayer of Western roles on the American stage."

Hart could have continued in the theater and retired after a long, successful career had he not stepped inside a Cleveland nickelodeon in 1913, where he saw a Western film that he claimed was "awful." Having spent so much of his youth in the West, Hart was appalled by what he saw on screen, which he felt was inauthentic to the point of insulting. Disgusted, he decided to become a Western actor in the new medium of film, with the intention of showing the West as it really was, not as he saw it depicted.

It was a bold step for Hart, since he was making the career change at the advanced age of 48. But like the gambler he would later play in some of his films, Hart beat the odds after contacting his old friend, producer Thomas Ince, who he had known from the theater. Ince had already moved west to become the head of the New York Motion Picture Company, where he created many of the now-familiar tropes of the Western film genre. He offered Hart $75 per week to come to California and appear in his own series of Westerns.

Hart made a series of two-reelers before starring in *The Bargain*, which was the catalyst that launched his career into the stratosphere. Now one of the biggest stars in Hollywood, Hart signed a 16-picture deal with Famous Players, a forerunner of what would later become Paramount Pictures, earning $150,000 per film plus a percentage of the profits. The first film he made at Famous Players was *The Narrow Trail*, which was most notable for teaming Hart with Fritz, a pinto pony who became so popular that he often received more fan mail than Hart.

In 1919, Hart nearly became one of the founders of United Artists alongside Charlie Chaplin, Mary Pickford, Douglas Fairbanks, and D.W. Griffith before dropping out of the proposed partnership. By that time, he was earning $250,000 for each film in addition to an astounding 75 percent of the gross receipts.

Hart often risked life and limb performing his own stunts. He regularly took falls with Fritz, tussled in barroom fights where no punches were pulled, and once made a 70-foot jump from a cliff into the water below—all in the name of entertainment. During the filming of *The Toll Gate* (1920), both Hart and Fritz nearly drowned filming a scene in a flooded cave.

In 1923, Hart signed a nine-picture contract with United Artists, but disputes with the producers saw the deal voided after only two movies were completed. Embittered and pushing 60, Hart decided to leave Hollywood behind after making one last film about the Oklahoma land rush. While undoubtedly one of his finest films, *Tumbleweeds* was a disappointment at the box office. Hart felt it was time to hang up his spurs and retire to his ranch in Newhall after completing his 11-year film career in which he acted in over 70 films, directed over 50 of them, produced 18, and scripted 11.

Something of a Lothario, Hart was famous for proposing to his leading ladies. While rebounding from a failed romance with actress Jane Novak, Hart married actress Winifred Westover when he was 57 and she was only 22. The marriage produced a son but was short-lived, reportedly due to tensions between Winifred and Hart's invalid sister Mary Ellen, who lived with her brother.

Hart first came to Horseshoe Ranch in 1918 to film a movie. Three years later, he purchased the property and eventually expanded it to over 200 acres. At that time, he lived with Mary Ellen in West Hollywood. The ranch house on Horseshoe Ranch's lower level became their residence on their frequent visits to the property. It would become their primary home while Hart's retirement home, La Loma de los Vientos ("The Hill of the Winds"), was being built further up the hill in a spot overlooking the sleepy village of Newhall. The 10,000-square-foot, seven-bath, 22-room mansion was constructed in the Spanish Colonial Revival style. It was designed by Los Angeles architect Arthur Kelly and built at a cost of $130,000. As much a museum as a residence, the property was decorated with Old West and Native American art, including paintings by Hart's friends Frederick Remington, Charlie Russell, and James Flagg. The latter had famously created the iconic Uncle Sam "I Want You!" recruiting poster during World War I. The mansion housed Hart's impressive gun collection and had a separate bedroom for his harlequin Great Danes. The property was graced with five statues, including a bronze of Hart and Fritz called *Range Rider of the Yellowstone* by Charles C. Christadoro, which was later used as a model for a much larger work in Billings, Montana.

Construction on the home began in December 1926, and Hart and Mary Ellen moved in a year later. It would serve as their home for the remainder of their lives. Today, the items inside the mansion are managed by the NHM.

During Hart's retirement, he wrote 11 books, including his autobiography, *My Life: East and West*. He also hosted a wide array of the era's most famous celebrities, including Wyatt Earp, Robert Taylor, Barbara Stanwyck, Will Rogers, Maurice Chevalier, and Amelia Earhart.

Injuries suffered during his many films plagued Hart during his final years. He was also deeply wounded by the deaths of friends Charles Russell, Wyatt Earp, Will Rogers, and his prized pinto Fritz. In 1943, he suffered a devastating blow when his sister and constant companion Mary Ellen died. Hart passed away only three years later at the age of 81.

As a final act of charity, Hart left Horseshoe Ranch to the County of Los Angeles to be used as a park and museum. He stated in his will that "when I was making pictures, the people gave me their nickels, dimes, and quarters. When I am gone, I want them to have my home." True to his word, Hart's Horseshoe Ranch, now known as William S. Hart Park, opened to the public on September 20, 1958.

In addition to the mansion, the park has several other notable structures. Visitors can see the bunkhouse, the ranch house, Hart Hall, Fritz's grave, the dog cemetery, the bookstore, the park office, and the Trading Post gift shop. Perhaps the park's most popular attraction is the animals. There is a large barnyard containing ducks, geese, horses, deer, rabbits, chickens, potbelly pigs, boars, alpacas, a turkey, a donkey, and a pair of tortoises named Bill and Mary Ellen. Closer to the mansion is a herd of a dozen American bison, some descended from those gifted to the park in the 1960s by Walt Disney.

Near Hart Hall is the entrance to Heritage Junction, which houses many of the most historic structures from Santa Clarita's past. Found here are the Saugus train station, the Newhall ranch house, the Pardee House, the Mitchell Adobe, and the Mogul locomotive engine No. 1629, which was donated to the park by Gene Autry. Also here is Quester Court, which consists of the Edison and Kingsburry houses, the Callahan schoolhouse, and the charming miniature Ramona Chapel. Each of these structures was moved here from other locations around the valley. Further on, at the far end of the park, there is even a campground.

Through the years, Hart Park has hosted hundreds of picnics, parties, weddings, and quinceañeras. It has also been the site of several festivals, including the Santa Clarita Cowboy Festival, Cowboys and Carols, Bow Wows & Meows, the Hart of the West Pow Wow, the Polynesian Festival, Silents Under the Stars, and the Newhallywood Silent Film Festival. Hart Park also serves as the headquarters for two volunteer organizations: the FOHP and the SCVHS.

Today, the beautiful, shady 265 acres of William S. Hart Park serve as a serene oasis amidst the bustling city of Santa Clarita. It also stands as a fitting testament to Hart's life, career, and generosity.

Bill West and E.J. and Kim Stephens
Winter 2021

One

William S. Hart

Prints in Cement. Grauman's Chinese Theatre (now the TCL Chinese Theater) is world-renowned for its forecourt featuring signatures and footprints of famous actors and actresses etched in cement. The tradition began with Douglas Fairbanks and Mary Pickford in April 1927. William S. Hart added his hand and boot prints in November of that same year along with impressions of his Two-Gun Bill pistols.

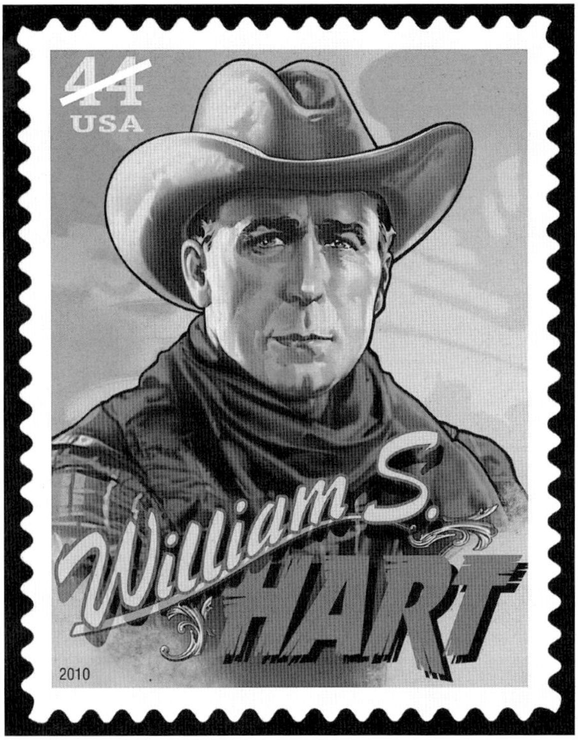

WILLIAM S. HART STAMP. In April 2010, the US Postal Service released a series of four stamps entitled Cowboys of the Silver Screen. Hart was memorialized along with Gene Autry, Roy Rogers, and Tom Mix. Hart's image was based on the movie poster for his final film, *Tumbleweeds*. A special ceremony to unveil the stamp was held outside Hart's mansion at William S. Hart Park, which was attended by representatives from the NHM, Los Angeles County Department of Parks and Recreation, FOHP, and the US Postal Service.

WILLIAM S. HART MAGAZINE COVER. Hart is an inspiration to late bloomers everywhere. He began as a stage actor in his 20s; began film acting—considered a risky career choice at the time—when he was pushing 50; and became an author in his 60s after retiring to his home in Newhall. (Courtesy of Roger and Becki Basham.)

Chief Plenty Coups. While traveling in the West with his father, Hart became a true friend to and fan of Native Americans and remained so for the rest of his life. He said, "There never lived a better-natured or finer man than the Indian." He was honored as a friend to the native peoples in Montana and Wyoming. He is pictured here with Chief Alaxchíia Ahú (Chief Plenty Coups), who was considered the last great Crow chief and worked with the US government to save Crow lands. He was the only Native American in attendance at the dedication of the Tomb of the Unknown Soldier following World War I. (Courtesy of Roger and Becki Basham.)

Stage Career. Many are surprised to learn that Hart's time on stage lasted longer than his film career. Pictured at left is Hart in the role of Messala, which he created for the 1899 Broadway play *Ben Hur*. Hart was performing in Cleveland as Judd Tolliver in the play *Trail of the Lonesome Pine* when he ducked into a nickelodeon and saw his first Western film. He was aghast at its inaccuracies, calling it a "burlesque." As he later wrote in his autobiography, that experience inspired him "to bend every endeavor to get a chance to make Western motion pictures." Below, Hart acts in a scene from the play *The Squaw Man*.

LIEBLER & CO.'S PRODUCTION OF "THE SQUAW MAN" ACT II. NAT-U-RITCH: "ME KILL HIM."

Early Film Career. Hart began his film career after he convinced his old acting buddy Thomas Ince, who was now producing movies in Santa Monica, to bring him to California to make his own kind of Westerns. Hart's extensive stage experience and insistence on realism soon propelled him to international stardom on screen. Hart is pictured here in the lost 1918 film *The Border Wireless* with his costar, Wanda Hawley, looking on. (Courtesy of Roger and Becki Basham.)

Movie Magazines. Two years into his film career, Hart appeared on the cover of *The Photoplay Weekly Mirror* with a caption that reads, "William S. Hart whose genius released the 'Western drama' from the yoke of mediocrity." Hart insisted on realism in his films. For example, it was standard procedure in Westerns to water down trails before filming to limit the dust. Hart felt this was inauthentic and banned the practice from his sets.

Fritz and Friends. Pictured here from left to right are Lisbeth the mule, Fritz the pinto pony, and Hart. Fritz could be a touchy actor and would only perform if Lisbeth and a mare named Cactus Kate were nearby. Fritz's grave may be visited in Hart Park, and Lisbeth has a hiking trail named after her behind the mansion. (Courtesy of Roger and Becki Basham.)

The Narrow Trail. Hart appeared with his pony pal Fritz in 1917's *The Narrow Trail*, which was the last time Fritz would be in a Hart film for the next two-and-a-half years—a span of 15 films. In *The Narrow Trail*, the pony is shunned by Hart's outlaw gang because they fear his unique markings could give them away to the authorities. Hart turns on the gang and heads out on his own, riding Fritz. In a case of life mirroring art, Hart's producer, Thomas Ince, who did not care for the pony, was responsible for Fritz's departure. By the time Fritz returned to the screen, Ince was no longer involved in Hart's movies.

Hart to Hart. Hart's 1921 flick *Three Word Brand* was named after "the Listenin'est Man in Utah," one of Hart's characters who was a taciturn fellow who rarely uttered more than three words. In the movie, Hart plays two brothers and their father. In the scene pictured here, the brothers meet and later clasp hands. This challenging cinematic effect was made possible by Hart's cameraman Joe August, who worked with Hart in over half of his films. August later co-founded the American Society of Cinematographers. *Three Word Brand* was the last time Hart co-starred with actress Jane Novak, his one-time girlfriend. (Courtesy of Roger and Becki Basham.)

MARY PICKFORD. Pictured with Hart (right) are Mary Pickford and her real-life brother, actor Jack Pickford. Jack battled alcoholism and died at age 36, while his sister Mary—along with her husband Douglas Fairbanks, Charlie Chaplin, and D.W. Griffith—founded United Artists in 1919. Hart was invited into the partnership but declined, fearing it would harm his relationship with Famous Players studio head Adolph Zukor.

LIBERTY BOND TOUR. Hart raised millions of dollars for the US government during World War I by appearing in a series of Liberty Loan bond drives and short promotional films. He was joined on the road by fellow Hollywood stars Mary Pickford, Douglas Fairbanks, and Charlie Chaplin. This image shows Hart speaking at a bond rally in New York. (Courtesy of Roger and Becki Basham.)

WHITE OAK. Pictured here are Vola Vale, Hart, and a clever dog named Jeff from the 1921 film *White Oak*, which Hart wrote, produced, and starred in. By 1921, Hart was making fewer films but spending more time and money on each production. *White Oak's* complex plot is centered around Hart's character's devotion to his sister (mirroring real life); her nurse being mistreated by a domineering father, prompting her brother to exact revenge; Hart taking the blame; and a subplot about a bad guy who kidnapped the daughter of an Indian chief—quite complex, indeed. And speaking of complex tales, in Hart's autobiography, he shares the equally twisted behind-the-scenes story of the making of this film, which involved the freezing Sacramento River, a trainload of wine, and the Victorville jail.

TRAVELIN' ON. Hart is pictured here reading a trade magazine on the set of 1922's *Travelin' On*. The film was based on a story written by Hart. The screenplay was penned by Lambert Hillyer, who worked with Hart on many films. The film stars Hart, his pony Fritz, and a monkey named Jocko. Fritz was not happy working with the monkey. Making matters worse, Fritz's favorite equine companions—Cactus Kate and the mule Lisbeth—were not allowed on set. Eventually, Cactus Kate was brought in and helped Fritz settle down. But havoc ensued when Lisbeth, feeling left out during filming, broke out of her stall and stormed the set. Ironically, Hart's character declares in the film, "Trust nothing but yourself and no one on less than four legs."

FRITZ. Here is a photograph of Hart with his prized pinto pony Fritz. Fritz's fans were dismayed when the horse disappeared from 15 of Hart's films. His absence was due to a disagreement between Hart and his producer, Thomas Ince. Hart later recalled, "For some unaccountable reason, Tom, who could always see anything that had a money value, could not see Fritz. He just did not like the horse, and I was never able to find out why." One likely reason was that Fritz was tiny in stature, and Hart stood tall at six foot two inches. As a result, sometimes a hole was dug for Hart to stand in, or occasionally Fritz was placed on a platform, so that their heights would look more natural on screen.

Sand. "Fritz is back" was the announcement made in 1920 when Hart's pinto returned to the screen after a two-year absence to costar in *Sand*. Hart sneaks in some fine drama in the film and even takes a pratfall for a bit of comedy. In one scene, he appears to dive off a cliff into a river on Fritz's back (using a stuffed likeness of the horse). Pres. Woodrow Wilson declared *Sand* to be his favorite Hart movie. Pictured here is Hart early in the film playing a railroad station agent. (Courtesy of Roger and Becki Basham.)

HAPPY HART. In this rare photograph is a laughing William S. Hart, who always played stoic, serious characters on screen. However, it is not rare to see him pictured near (or on) his pony Fritz. Hart once said of Fritz, "He weighed only one thousand pounds, but his power and endurance were remarkable." Hart dearly loved Fritz, and so did his fans, who often sent more mail to the pony than to Bill.

LAUGHING HART. Fritz's fan mail sometimes included sugar cubes for the pony. His fans loved Fritz like their children would later cherish Gene Autry's horse Champion and Roy Rogers's horse Trigger. Fritz retired with Bill to Horseshoe Ranch, and when the pinto pony passed away in 1938, Hart was heartbroken. He said at the time, "I'd give both my shoes—with my feet in them—to have him back." Hart buried Fritz on the property, and folks can still visit his grave at Hart Park.

Hart and Horses. Hart had several horses at Horseshoe Ranch who could often be seen grazing in front of his mansion. This image shows Hart with some of his equine pals from later in his life. The donkey on the left is probably Tuffy and the horse on the right is likely King Valentine. In addition to leaving his home and the rest of what is today William S. Hart Park to his fans in his will, Hart made provisions for the one horse that outlived him, a gray gelding named Old Roaney, insuring he could live out his days at the park. Old Roaney, who outlived Hart by more than 20 years, died at age 45 in 1968.

Winifred Westover. In Hart's autobiography, Winifred Westover gets only a single mention in its 350-plus pages, which is telling since Westover, for a short time, was Hart's wife! She starred with Hart in the 1919 movie *John Petticoats*. Their relationship ended after a few months, but their brief union produced one happy result—the birth of their son, William S. Hart Jr.

Anne of Little Smoky. This is a lobby card from a 1921 lost silent film called *Anne of Little Smoky*, which starred Winifred Westover and was released two weeks before she became Mrs. William S. Hart. It has been speculated that Westover was a rebound relationship after Hart's engagement with actress Jane Novak ended and that Hart's live-in sister Mary Ellen never bonded with his new wife. Neither Hart nor Westover ever married again.

Bill Hart Jr. William S. Hart Jr. graduated from the University of California, Los Angeles with a master's degree in environmental planning. During World War II, he worked as a cryptographer for the Office of Strategic Services in Washington, DC. He later became a Santa Monica real estate appraiser and also taught business at the University of Southern California and UCLA. Hart Jr. had three daughters and died in 2004 at the age of 81, the same age as his father.

Hart Jr. and Westover. William S. Hart Jr. and his mother, Winifred Westover, prepare for a court appearance in an unsuccessful attempt to overrule Hart's will. Hart had left his Horseshoe Ranch property and home in Newhall to the County of Los Angeles and his West Hollywood home to the City of Los Angeles. Westover and Hart Jr. believed they should inherit the properties, claiming Hart was not of sound mind at the time he made his will.

Penny Farthing Bicycle. Hart is pictured here with Barbara Bedford, his costar in his final film, 1925's *Tumbleweeds*. Hart sits atop a popular early bicycle called the penny-farthing. Its name comes from the difference in sizes of the two wheels, which was reminiscent of two British coins of the time, the penny (large) and the farthing (small). The large wheel made fast travel possible, but the design was dangerous. The development of gears and air-filled tires soon spelled the end of the penny-farthing because these improvements solved its primary problem: the likelihood of injury when the rider fell off. The bicycle is featured in the film because the real-life 1893 Oklahoma land rush depicted in *Tumbleweeds* included "sooners" traveling on all forms of transportation, including the penny-farthing.

TUMBLEWEEDS. Above, Hart, at age 60, strikes a classic pose in a publicity still from his 1925 silent epic *Tumbleweeds.* Hart's swan song is considered by most critics to be his finest film, and one of the best silent movies ever made. It tells a heartfelt and action-packed story of the Oklahoma territory land rush. *Tumbleweeds* was Hart's last starring role, but he did show up again on the screen briefly in *Show People* (1928) starring Marion Davies. Surprisingly, *Show People* was a comedy and Hart played it for laughs. He again returned to the big screen in 1939—seven years shy of his death—in an eight-minute spoken prologue for the re-release of *Tumbleweeds.* This was the first time many Hart fans ever heard his voice.

Ruiz Cemetery. Throughout his retirement, Hart was anything but aloof and kept actively involved in local happenings. Soon after the nearby St. Francis Dam break in 1928, Hart and a group of his cowboy friends erected a stone marker dedicated to the victims of the disaster. Among the dead were eight members of the Ruiz family of San Francisquito Canyon. The memorial marker and graves of the unfortunate Ruiz clan can still be viewed today in the Ruiz Cemetery, just a few miles downstream from the former dam site.

American Legion Hall. Despite having one of the world's most famous movie stars as a resident, Newhall had no movie theater. Hart was determined to solve this problem, so in 1940, he donated property and funds so that the town could finally have a theater of its own. His only request was that it feature at least one Western every week. The theater continued to show movies until 1965, when a larger one was built in town. Today, the former theater is only a short walk from William S. Hart Park and serves as the American Legion Post 507.

On The Air. During the lead-up to America's involvement in World War II, there were concerns that the European fascist nations might try to sway Latin American countries to join the Axis powers, placing enemies at America's doorstep. Several entertainers, including Hart, were engaged to create goodwill with Central and South American audiences to help foster solidarity during the war. In the 1941 photograph above, translator Arthur Deter (left) and NBC International broadcaster John Barrett (right) flank Hart, who is demonstrating how Two-Gun Bill used his pistols during an NBC radio show that was broadcast south of the border. At left, Hart (right) appears with vaudeville comic Charlie Mack, who lived down the hill from Hart in Newhall. Mack died in a car accident in Arizona less than a year after this photograph was taken.

Lina Basquette. Disembarking from a train in Hollywood in 1932 are Hart and Lina Basquette. These two stars had quite different ideas about matrimony. While Hart was married only once, Basquette was married a total of eight times: five ending in divorce, two in death, and one in annulment. Her first marriage was to Sam Warner, one of the four Warner brothers. After his death, she lost custody of their daughter to the Warner family in a bitter legal dispute. At the time of this photograph, Basquette had married boxer Jack Dempsey's personal trainer, who, it turned out, was already married to someone else—this coming after her torrid and very public affair with Dempsey. After the trainer's divorce, Basquette married him again for real. One thing she did have in common with Hart was a love of Great Danes, which she raised for many years.

VALENTINO, HART, AND FAIRBANKS. The above photograph was taken at a 1925 Shriners convention where 100,000 Shriners descended upon Los Angeles, many of them in Pullman cars like the one seen in the background. Three of the era's most popular celebrities of the silver screen are pictured here: (from left to right) Rudolph Valentino, William S. Hart, and Douglas Fairbanks. All three men were members of the Shriners, an organization that engages in charitable endeavors. Below, Hart is seated with two women at a horse racetrack.

FREDDIE BARTHOLOMEW. In this 1935 photograph, Hart is on hand in Hollywood to greet British child actor Freddie Bartholomew, who had recently starred in the title role of the 1935 MGM film *David Copperfield*. Here, he is dressed in a cowboy costume, proving that long after Hart's final feature film, he was still a well-known star who up-and-coming actors were thrilled to meet.

OUR GANG. Hart is pictured around 1930 horsing around with the *Our Gang/The Little Rascals* kids. The members shown are believed to be, from left to right, Bobby "Wheezer" Hutchins, Donald Haines, Joe Cobb, Mary Ann Jackson, Jean Darling (astride Hart), Norman "Chubby" Chaney, Pete the Pup, and Alan "Farina" Hoskins. The *Our Gang* comedies, which started out as silent shorts, featured sound at the time of this photograph. Hart was said to be in talks with *Our Gang* producer Hal Roach about making a "talkie" Western. Unfortunately, this never happened.

Charlie Mack House. At left in 1933 are comedian Charlie Mack and Hart in front of Mack's house in Newhall. When Mack died in an automobile accident the following year, Hart attended the funeral held in the living room of this home and led the mourners in prayer while kneeling next to the casket. Later, the home was rented by Mack's friend, comedian W.C. Fields. Below at Charlie Mack's house are, from left to right, actor Wallace Beery Sr., Hart, Mack's comedy teammate George Moran, and Mack. Mack owned three homes on Eighth Street, which collectively became known as "Crowland" in reference to Mack and Moran's comedy duo, the Two Black Crows.

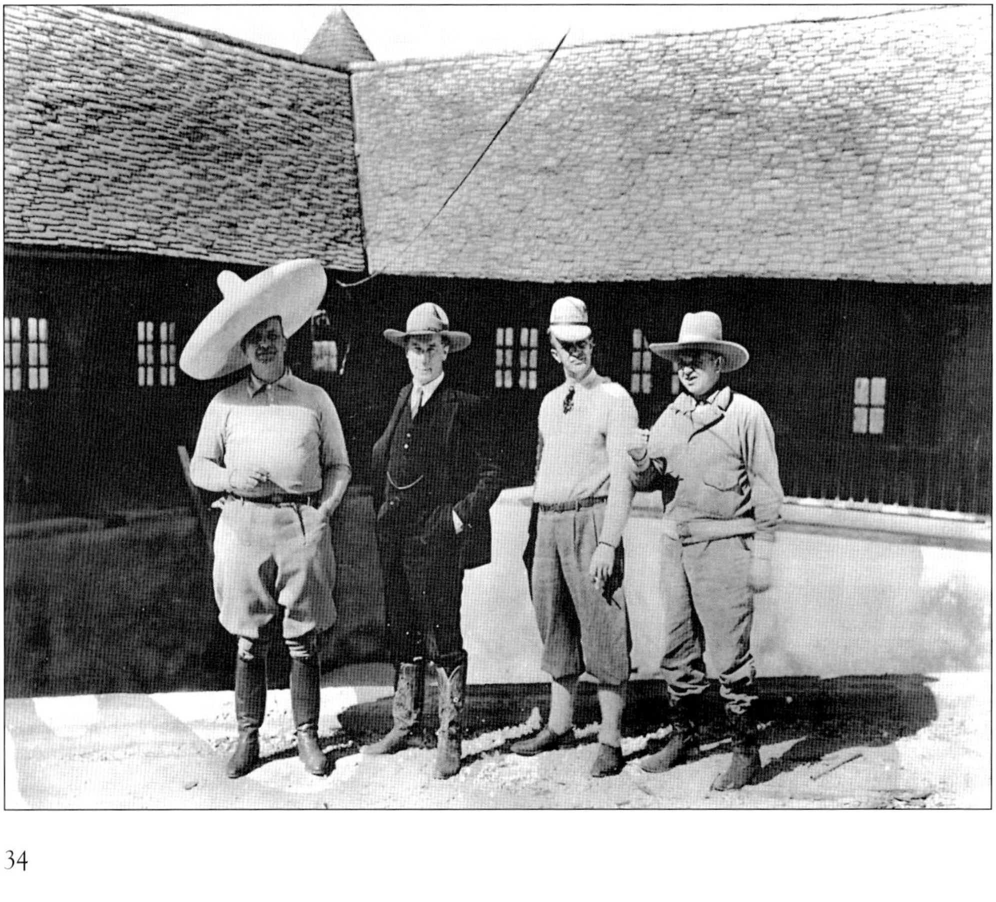

FRITZ'S GRAVE. Hart first saw Fritz when the small pinto horse appeared in an early Western film at Thomas Ince's huge "Inceville" studio on the Malibu coast. Impressed with the intelligence and strength of the horse, Fritz became Hart's primary mount and a fan favorite. Fritz retired from filmmaking in 1924 after the release of *Singer Jim McKee* and lived out the rest of his life at Horseshoe Ranch, passing away on February 6, 1938. Hart said Fritz was "the finest friend I ever had." (E.J. Stephens.)

ROBERT TAYLOR. William S. Hart is shown chatting with actor Robert Taylor at Fritz's grave. Taylor was visiting Hart's home with his wife, actress Barbara Stanwyck. Taylor was preparing for his first Western role, that of Billy the Kid, in the 1941 movie of the same name. Hart owned what was said to be a pistol owned by the real Billy the Kid and Taylor may actually have used it in some scenes in the movie. During the visit, Hart presented Taylor and Stanwyck with a Charlie Russell painting and autographed copies of his books.

HART, TAYLOR, AND STANWYCK. Famous actors William S. Hart, Barbara Stanwyck, and her husband, Robert Taylor, are seen here in the backyard of Hart's mansion, with harlequin Great Danes Prince Hamlet and Princess Galatia bringing up the rear. Hart was thrilled to have the actors pay him a visit, which was planned as part of Taylor's preparation for his first Western, *Billy The Kid*. The movie was completed in 1941, five years before Hart's death.

COUPLES IN THE LIVING ROOM. In this undated photograph, Hart and an unidentified woman entertain a couple believed to be Ethel Rose James, the granddaughter of train robber Jesse James, and bandleader Jay Whidden (in the white hat) in the living room of Hart's retirement mansion.

Charlie Russell. Famed Western artist Charlie Russell is seen here with Hart. Russell painted Hart for the cover of his autobiography, *My Life: East and West*, and actually saw Hart perform on stage long before his 1914 film debut. Even though they worked in different creative fields, they were kindred spirits when it came to their love of the Old West. A tour of Hart's home is like visiting a Charlie Russell museum since so many pieces of his artwork are found there. (Courtesy of Roger and Becki Basham.)

TEN-MILLIONTH MODEL T. The past meets the future in this photograph. In 1924, at the end of a successful Western film career in which he invariably appeared atop a horse, Hart poses with a technological milestone, the ten-millionth Ford Model T. The car had recently come off the Detroit assembly line and was making a cross-country tour from New York, stopping at Hart's ranch on its way to San Francisco. A visit to Hart's home reveals that the actor, who always glorified the past on screen, was nevertheless a fan of modern technology, including a foot-operated intercom system, an early record changer, and a fleet of his own automobiles. In the background of the photograph is the ranch house, Hart's temporary home as his mansion was being built atop the hill. Visitors to the park can tour this structure.

MAURICE CHEVALIER. Bill Hart is shown here giving a few shooting pointers to fellow actor Maurice Chevalier, the famous Parisian singer and entertainer, who is atypically outfitted in cowboy gear, which he was said to have borrowed from Hart. Below, Hart shows off his six-shooter to some young fans. Hart was a very personable man who related the same to his famous fans as to his unknown ones, whatever their age.

Hart and Earhart. Sometime around 1934, a plane buzzed Hart's home in Newhall. He claimed the noise "Damn near shook the bricks out of the chimney." He went outside and wrote down the plane's tail number and called the sheriff. He was shocked to learn that the plane turned out to belong to famous aviatrix Amelia Earhart. Fast forward to 1936, when Earhart visited Hart at Horseshoe Ranch. Hart gave Earhart a signed copy of his autobiography and a historic buffalo coat. In return, Earhart gave Hart a small American flag she carried on a flight across the Atlantic. Sadly, this was probably the last time the two saw each other, as Earhart disappeared during her around-the-world journey the following year. Below, Hart shows Robert Taylor the flag given to him by Earhart.

WYATT EARP. Hart not only had actor friends who played famous Old West heroes, but he was also a friend to real Old West heroes like Bat Masterson and gunfighter Wyatt Earp, who is seen in this photograph. On a tour of the mansion at Hart Park, visitors will see photographs of both lawmen and a "quirt" (a noise-making whip used to guide horses) given to Hart by Earp. A letter from Earp accompanied the gift claiming the quirt was made by a woman serving a life sentence for killing her husband. Earp and Hart shared mutual respect, and the lawman hoped Hart would pen his biography and set the record straight on his exploits. There was also talk of Hart playing Earp in a film. Both men were enthusiastic about the projects, but sadly, Earp passed away in Los Angeles in 1929 before either could get underway. Hart and fellow cowboy star Tom Mix served as pallbearers at Earp's funeral.

Autobiography. Hart is seen here putting the finishing touches on his autobiography, *My Life: East and West*, while in Chicago. Thanks to the members of FOHP, especially Bill Crowl and Becki and Roger Basham, the autobiography has been reprinted and is available for purchase at the park's gift store, the Trading Post. First published in 1929 with cover art from a painting by famed Western artist Charlie Russell, Hart's autobiography is still the primary source of data on the actor's life.

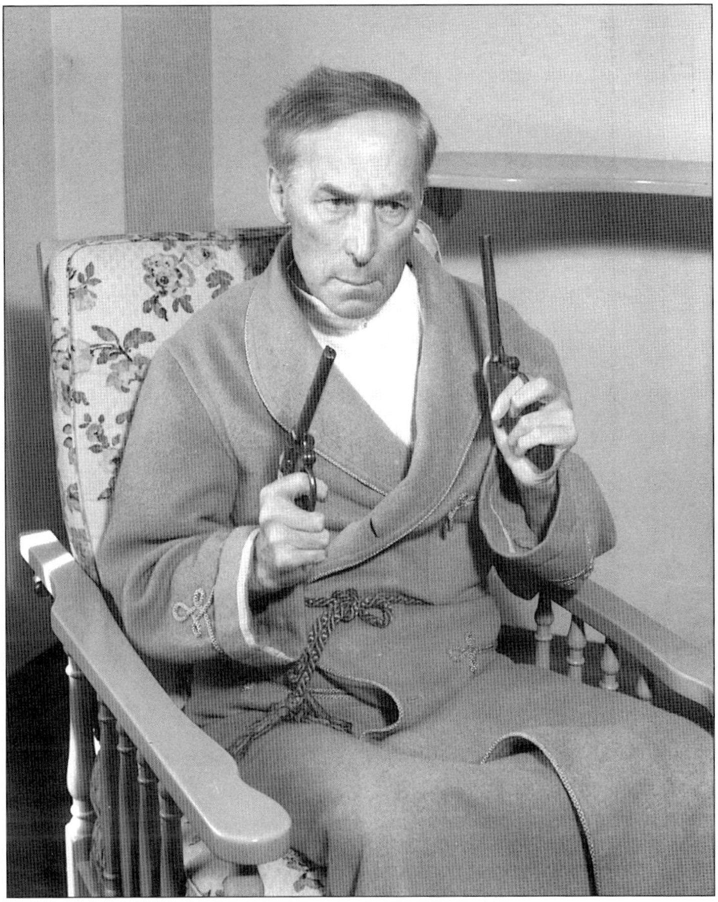

The Final Photograph. This last known photograph of William S. Hart was taken in 1946, less than six months before his death. He displays the legendary skill with twin pistols that made him famous as Two-Gun Bill. Hart's legacy lives on in his surviving films, his writings, and in Hart Park. The staff members and volunteers at the William S. Hart Park and Museum—most of whom were born long after Hart's death—continue to dedicate countless hours helping to keep this portion of his legacy alive.

Newhall. This is the view of Newhall that Hart would have seen from atop his property during his final years. At the time Hart moved to Horseshoe Ranch, only a few hundred people lived in Newhall. Today, the town is a district of the city of Santa Clarita, with nearly a quarter-million inhabitants.

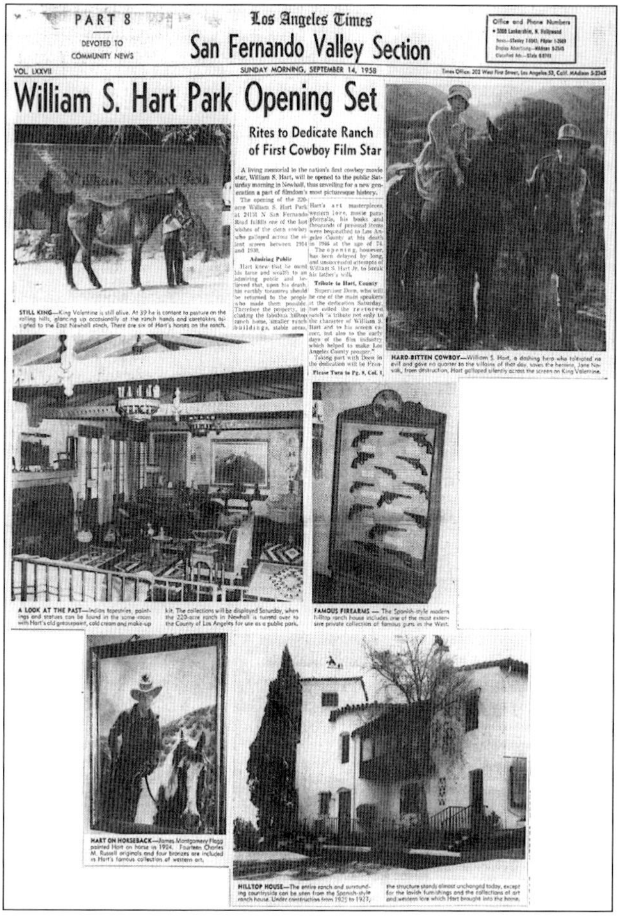

PART 8
DEVOTED TO COMMUNITY NEWS

Los Angeles Times
San Fernando Valley Section

Office and Phone Numbers
• 5000 Lankershim, N. Hollywood

VOL. LXXVII — SUNDAY MORNING, SEPTEMBER 14, 1958 — Times Office: 202 West First Street, Los Angeles 53, Calif. MAdison 5-2345

William S. Hart Park Opening Set

Rites to Dedicate Ranch of First Cowboy Film Star

A living memorial to the nation's first cowboy movie star, William S. Hart, will be opened to the public Saturday morning in Newhall, thus unveiling for a new generation a part of filmdom's most picturesque history.

The opening of the 220-acre William S. Hart Park at 24151 N San Fernando Road fulfills one of the last wishes of the stern cowboy who galloped across the silent screen between 1914 and 1930.

Admiring Public

Hart knew that he owed his fame and wealth to an admiring public and believed that, upon his death, his earthly treasures should be returned to the people who made them possible. Therefore the property, including the fabulous hilltop ranch home, smaller ranch buildings, stable areas, Hart's art masterpieces, western lore, movie paraphernalia, his books and thousands of personal items were bequeathed to Los Angeles County at his death in 1946 at the age of 74.

The opening, however, has been delayed by long, and unsuccessful attempts of William S. Hart Jr. to break his father's will.

Tribute to Hart, County

Supervisor Dorn, who will be one of the main speakers at the dedication Saturday, has called the restored ranch "a tribute not only to the character of William S. Hart and to his screen career, but also to the early days of the film industry which helped to make Los Angeles County prosper."

Taking part with Dorn in the dedication will be Fran-

Please Turn to Pg. 8, Col. 1

STILL KING—King Valentine is still alive. At 39 he is content to pasture on the rolling hills, glancing up occasionally at the ranch hands and caretakers assigned to the East Newhall ranch. There are six of Hart's horses on the ranch.

HARD-BITTEN COWBOY—William S. Hart, a dashing hero who tolerated no evil and gave no quarter to the villains of that day, saves the heroine, Jane Novak, from destruction. Hart galloped silently across the screen on King Valentine.

A LOOK AT THE PAST—Indian tapestries, paintings and statues can be found in the same room with Hart's old greasepaint, cold cream and make-up kit. The collections will be displayed Saturday, when the 220-acre ranch in Newhall is turned over to the County of Los Angeles for use as a public park.

FAMOUS FIREARMS — The Spanish-style modern hilltop ranch house includes one of the most extensive private collection of famous guns in the West.

HART ON HORSEBACK—James Montgomery Flagg painted Hart on horse in 1924. Fourteen Charles M. Russell originals and four bronzes are included in Hart's famous collection of western art.

HILLTOP HOUSE—The entire ranch and surrounding countryside can be seen from the Spanish-style ranch house. Under construction from 1925 to 1927, the structure stands almost unchanged today, except for the lavish furnishings and the collections of art and western lore which Hart brought into the home.

HART PARK DEDICATION. Celebrities and politicians gathered at the dedication ceremony of William S. Hart Park in Newhall on Saturday, September 20, 1958. In attendance were Sheriff Eugene Biscailuz, actor Guinn "Big Boy" Williams, Los Angeles county supervisor Warren Dorn, silent film actor Francis X. Bushman, actor Leo Carillo, Los Angeles county supervisor John Anson Ford, rodeo trick rider Montie Montana, and Francis Gudger, the husband of silent film actress Marjorie Burnet Rambea. The plaque seen below is encased in a wall near the front door of the mansion. (Left, courtesy of scvhistory.com; below, courtesy of Ken Lubas.)

Two

THE MANSION

PLAQUE AT MANSION. In 1921, Bill Hart purchased the small five-acre Horseshoe Ranch from George Babcock Smith and immediately began buying up adjoining properties whenever they became available. By 1925, Hart had retired from acting and decided to move from West Hollywood to his ranch in Newhall to live out his remaining years. Construction began there on his retirement mansion in late 1926. Just as he did at Hollywood's Chinese Theatre courtyard in 1927, Hart wrote his name and placed his six-shooters in cement behind the mansion the following year. (Courtesy of Ken Lubas.)

WEST HOLLYWOOD HOME. There is another William S. Hart Park in Southern California at Hart's former home in West Hollywood. Hart donated this land to the city on his passing, and it serves as a dog park, among other uses. This is particularly appropriate since Hart was a dog lover. The sign quotes Hart from 1944: "I would like to say in all sincerity of which I am capable that in donating this beautiful spot . . . my former home, I am only trying to do an act of justice. I am only trying to give back to the American public some part of what the American public has already given to me." The 3,000 square-foot home on DeLongpre Avenue is where Hart lived when he was making motion pictures. He was such a big star that the view of his home seen below was made into a postcard. After Hart's death, his home and property became the west coast branch of Lee Strasberg's famous acting school, the Actor's Studio.

Horseshoe Ranch. In July 1926, Hart wrote to architect Arthur Kelly, "I am contemplating building a Spanish-style home on my ranch in Newhall. Would you care to take a trip up there to look the location over and see if you would care to submit plans?" Kelly was subsequently hired to design the home to fit the contours of the mountain top so that the main living areas would be on the second floor and accessible at ground level from the backyard and garage area. The living room, bedrooms, and baths were situated on the upper level, with special consideration for exposure and airflow. As Hart's younger sister Mary required a wheelchair for mobility, the element of easy entry onto this floor was most important. This aerial photograph from 1963, looking toward the south, shows the entire ranch with the mansion on top of the hill to the right and the older portions of the property on the flatlands below. (Courtesy of Roger and Becki Basham.)

Mansion Design and Construction. Plans were drafted for a 10,000 square-foot, two-story home in the Spanish Colonial Revival style, which featured thick adobe-type walls, low-pitched tile roofs, beamed ceilings, white walls, arches, large fireplaces, and ample windows and doors for cross-ventilation. In total, there would be 22 rooms, including seven bathrooms, and a total of 7,500 square feet of living space with the remainder for storage. The undated photograph above shows the mansion under construction. The later image below shows it nearing completion.

Mansion. Construction of the mansion began in 1926 and was completed at the end of 1927. The cost for the structure is estimated to have been between $100,000 and $130,000. Soon after its completion, Hart and his sister moved into La Loma de los Vientos—"The Hill of the Winds"—where they would spend the remaining years of their lives. Seen here are images of the completed home viewed from the front and rear. (Both, courtesy of Roger and Becki Basham.)

La Loma de los Vientos. Visitors to the mansion enter through this door, just as Hart's guests did from 1927 until his death in 1946. Today, the mansion looks very much like it did when Hart was living here, and unlike many historic homes, this one is filled with the actual belongings of its former owner.

FLOATING STAIRCASE. Just inside the front door is the foyer, which features this floating staircase made from a single pouring of cement. The staircase was designed so that each step would support the weight of the one above it. It has survived many California earthquakes with no damage. Walking through Hart's home is a step back into the past, with a peek at the advanced technology of the time, including the staircase. (Courtesy of Roger and Becki Basham.)

FOYER. The floating staircase leads to the main living area of the house on the second floor. Note the swords and shield mounted above the arched doorways. These are relics from Hart's stage career. Another interesting feature is the dual staircase banister. The original banister was built low so Mary Ellen could see over the top rail from her wheelchair. The County of Los Angeles later added the taller railing for safety purposes. (Courtesy of Roger and Becki Basham.)

Artwork. A visit to Hart's mansion in Hart Park is not simply entering a former home, but stepping into an art museum. Paintings and sculptures by legendary artists like Frederic Remington, James Montgomery Flagg, and Charles Cristadoro are found throughout the mansion. But perhaps the most prominent artist represented in the house is Hart's good friend Charlie Russell. Hart first met Russell in Montana in 1902 during his stage-acting days. Russell was impressed with Hart's acting, but later referred to him as that "feller who doesn't talk none." Hart was equally impressed with the artwork that Russell created, which he felt captured the true spirit of the Old West. They began swapping letters between Montana and New York and eventually visited one another. By the time Hart retired to Newhall, Russell and his wife, Nancy, had become frequent visitors. Their relationship is forever joined in a literary sense as well: Charlie Russell's painting of William S. Hart graces the cover of Hart's autobiography. (Courtesy of Roger and Becki Basham.)

HART AND FLAGG. Hart and artist James Montgomery Flagg stand on each side of Flagg's painting of Hart atop Fritz. Flagg had wanted to paint them for some time and in 1924 drove across the country to Hart's Horseshoe Ranch to make it happen. Hart loved the idea, but Fritz got bored standing still for so long. Ultimately, Hart and Flagg moved to Hart's West Hollywood home, where he finished Fritz from memory, and painted Hart as he posed atop a whiskey barrel stacked on sawhorses. This original work now hangs in a place of honor in Hart's dining room. In the living room is another Flagg portrait of Hart's sister Mary Ellen with her cat Westport Pouffins. Flagg was famous for painting the Uncle Sam "I Want You" World War I recruitment poster.

Living Room. The Heinsbergen Galleries created the interior design for the mansion. Their touches can still be seen in the hand-painted motifs on the ceilings, beams, and doors, along with the complementing furnishings of rugs, Native American artifacts, and Western-themed artwork. The furnishings in the mansion are original, with a Native American influence pervading nearly every room. More than 20 artists—many of them friends of Hart—have their work placed throughout the home. The massive 24-by-48-foot living room features many windows that offer an excellent view of the surrounding hills. A large fireplace provided warmth during chilly winter months. Navajo rugs cover the floor along with a massive Kodiak bear rug, which was a gift from Will Rogers. A piano and combination phonograph/radio Electrola provided entertainment. Museum-quality paintings by Charlie Russell and other artists are displayed throughout the room. Movies were shown from a hidden projection booth on a drop-down screen with a 35-mm Simplex movie projector. (Courtesy of Roger and Becki Basham.)

ELECTROLA. One of the first of its kind, this Victor Talking Machine Company Electrola could play multiple stacked vinyl records. A commonplace item in later decades, at the time, it was a modern marvel. The Electrola had a purchase price of $1,350, which was said to have been the cost of two modest homes in the town of Newhall at the time. The "books" built into the device are actually vinyl record holders, again marrying high-tech gadgetry with a look that fits with the historic tone of the house. What certainly does not fit the home's Western style are the two 17th-century Japanese Samurai swords atop the Electrola. These were gifts to Hart from Dick and Ina Ito, a Japanese couple who were part of Hart's live-in staff. (Courtesy of Roger and Becki Basham.)

Display Case. In an efficient use of space, this display case was built into the wall. The plaster figurine of Hart and Fritz on the top shelf was fashioned by artist Charles A. Beil and is flanked by woodcarvings by Gene Hoback. The second shelf contains carvings by famous Western artist Charlie Russell, surrounding a book of his letters to friends. Russell's book is opened to a page showing a letter he sent to Hart. The third shelf has a collection of the books written by Hart and his sister while living in this house, supported by bookends given to Hart by his friend Joe McNinch, later a park volunteer. The bottom shelf contains Charlie Russell bronzes surrounding a photograph of Russell at work in his log cabin studio in Great Falls, Montana. (Courtesy of Roger and Becki Basham.)

Montana Sculpture. Speaking of Montana, Hart was honored with this statue in Billings in 1927. The sculpture was made by Charles Cristadoro, and on hand for the dedication ceremony were none other than Hart himself, along with Fritz. (Courtesy of scvhistory.com.)

Living Room, 1948. The NHM is tasked with overseeing the items inside the mansion. Although some of Hart's belongings have been stored offsite for historic preservation purposes, the NHM staff keeps the home looking much as it did when Hart lived here. This photograph, which was taken two years after Hart's passing, shows a portion of his extensive Navajo rug collection, which can be found throughout the home. (Courtesy of Roger and Becki Basham.)

Dining Room. On the ground floor, just off the entrance foyer, is the formal dining room, which had a long table for entertaining dinner guests. The feature on the outside wall that looks like a fireplace is actually a food warmer, which supplied heat from a wood fire below the support grill. At the far end of the dining room is the breakfast nook. The paintings in the room are by Robert Lambdin, Joe de Yong, and James Montgomery Flagg. (Courtesy of Roger and Becki Basham.)

HORSESHOES. Hart's horseshoe collection is prominently displayed on a wall in the dining room. Fritz's shoe is at the top on a heart-shaped plaque. Below, and to the far left on the middle row, is the shoe of Lisbeth the Mule, which has a different shape compared to Fritz's shoe. This is because horseshoes are curved inwards at the top, while the ends of a mule's shoe are more U-shaped. (Courtesy of Roger and Becki Basham.)

DINING ROOM DETAILS. Here is a closer look at Hart's formal dining room. Its table is graced by his collection of Czechoslovakian china. A hidden feature at the head of the table is a secret foot switch by which Hart could summon the kitchen staff. The food warmer, which resembles a fireplace, was discovered by Mary Ellen in an issue of *Vogue* magazine. (Courtesy of Roger and Becki Basham.)

I WANT YOU! Adjacent to the dining room is this small breakfast nook where Bill and Mary Ellen enjoyed private meals together. The architecture of the home features arched doorways for use by visitors and regular, rectangular doors for the staff. The painting on the far wall is of early American patriot Patrick Henry. It was painted by famous illustrator James Montgomery Flagg for the cover of Hart's book *The Lighter of Flames*, which was about the life of Henry. Many of the paintings throughout the mansion were actually commissioned as illustrations for the books Hart and his sister authored. Flagg is most famous for painting Uncle Sam for an iconic World War I recruiting poster. Below, the poster has been updated to remind everyone about social distancing during the COVID-19 pandemic. (Right, courtesy of Roger and Becki Basham; below, courtesy of VintageImageryX.)

KITCHEN. The mansion's kitchen is filled with original 1920s-era utensils and appliances. The clown-shaped citrus juicer seen near the center above was a gift to Hart from his son, Bill Hart Jr. It is a special treat visiting the mansion during the holidays when the museum staff and volunteers do an amazing job of decorating the entire house. At that time of year, the oven seen here is open, with holiday cookies on display. At left is the kitchen's original icebox. (Both, courtesy of Roger and Becki Basham.)

HART'S BEDROOM. Pictured here is Hart's second bedroom, which he added on to the house in 1937 after he donated his original, larger bedroom to his dogs. Hart's small bed makes us all scratch our heads a bit since he was six foot two inches tall, which must have forced him to sleep diagonally. A painting of Fritz holds a place of honor above the headboard. Hart's new bedroom served as both his bedroom and office. Throughout the room are several pictures of his horses and of his son William S. Hart Jr. Visitors peering into the adjoining bathroom can sometimes see Hart's wool bathing suit, as the items on display change throughout the year. (Both, courtesy of Roger and Becki Basham.)

Mary Ellen's Bedroom. In the background is the bedroom of Hart's beloved sister Mary Ellen, who cared for their dying parents when Bill was young. Her wheelchair can be seen here. She was injured in a car accident on the way to see her brother on a movie set, and was often confined to the wheelchair. Frequently on display is the carrier for Mary's cat Westport Pouffins. Like Bill, Mary Ellen was an animal lover and donated money in her will to a Westport, Connecticut, animal shelter. Her large bedroom sits on the front corner of the home and features a beautiful Monterey-style wood balcony, which is viewable from the front of the house. The room includes two closets, a bathroom, a fireplace, and a second balcony. Unlike her brother, Mary Ellen's tastes did not run toward Western décor, and her room is the only one in the house lacking a Western influence. (Courtesy of Roger and Becki Basham.)

Mary Ellen. Here is a portrait of Bill's sister Mary Ellen with her beloved cat Westport Pouffins. The painting was made two years after her death by James Montgomery Flagg using a photograph of them taken on the lawn of the house. Mary Ellen made frequent trips to Santa Monica during the hot Newhall summer months, and it was there at the Miramar Hotel that she passed away, apparently of a stroke. Hart was devastated by the loss of his sister. Westport Pouffins was likely named after Westport, Connecticut, the location of the home Bill bought for his mother and Mary Ellen while he traveled the stage circuit.

Dog's Bedroom. One of the more interesting bedrooms in the mansion was for the use of Hart's two Harlequin Great Danes. It began as Hart's bedroom but was turned over to his two dogs in 1937 when another bedroom was added for him. As was the custom throughout the house, several photographs and paintings decorate the room. Hart favored the dog's room as a place to relax, and frequently brought his guests here. (Courtesy of Roger and Becki Basham.)

COURTYARD. Visitors to the mansion enter on the first floor and exit through this door on the second floor. Above this door stands an observation tower. Visitors exiting the house can descend down an outdoor staircase to the lower level or, better yet, take a stroll along the mansion's driveway, which provides a view of the garage/chauffer's quarters and swimming pool. The window in the photograph is that of the dog's bedroom. Below is a view of the back porch. Hart built the benches himself out of local wood. (Both, courtesy of Roger and Becki Basham.)

SUNDECK. Opposite the garage on the west side of the driveway is the flagstone-covered sundeck. A small tearoom sits immediately inside the entrance. This location offers a great view to the west and provided Bill and Mary Ellen with a wonderful spot for outside entertaining and for spending leisure time. (Courtesy of Roger and Becki Basham.)

GATE TOWER. At the entrance gate to the mansion is this circular frame and stucco tower topped by a flagpole. The design allowed one to enter through a small wooden door and climb to the observation area. Due to deterioration, the tower is now closed to visitors. (Courtesy of Roger and Becki Basham.)

Pool and Pool House. Behind the mansion are the combination garage and chauffer's quarters. At various times, Hart owned a 1931 Ford Phaeton Deluxe four-door, a 1931 Studebaker sedan, a very exclusive 1928 Chrysler Roadster, the popular 1928 Model A Roadster, a 1922 Cadillac Touring car, and a 1923 Lincoln limousine. Below the mansion on the north side of the hill is the pool and pool house (pictured here), which were designed by Arthur Kelley and built in 1928. A flagstone patio was built around the swimming pool, and a semi-circular wood-frame and stucco building was erected to serve as changing rooms. After the park opened in 1958, the pool was filled in as a safety precaution. (Courtesy of Ken Lubas.)

Bunkhouse. The bunkhouse is on a trail leading up from the ranch house to the mansion. The original log cabin bunkhouse is thought to have been a movie set built for the Hart film *The Testing Block* (1920). It was destroyed in a fire in 1926. A new stucco bunkhouse was later built, which consists of one large room with a fireplace and a small bathroom. An outside entrance leads to a basement. Below is a photograph of Hart by the original wooden bunkhouse. This image may have been taken from Hart's 1924 feature *Singer Jim McKee*, which was likely partially filmed at the bunkhouse. Hart allowed people down on their luck during the Depression to stay in this building. It is also said that Hart would stray down to the bunkhouse to play poker with his ranch hands since Mary Ellen would not allow it in the main house. (Both, courtesy of Roger and Becki Basham.)

Dog Graveyard. Along the trail leading up to the bunkhouse is the dog graveyard. Hart had a deep love for his animals and was a strong supporter of the Society for the Prevention of Cruelty to Animals and the Humane Society. Both he and Mary Ellen left money in their wills for animal protection. Bill seemed to favor two breeds of canines: English bulldogs and Great Danes. The graveyard originally had wood headstones for each of his dogs, but over time, they were replaced with concrete monuments. Hart's beloved English bulldog Mack was originally buried at Inceville, his first movie ranch in the Santa Monica Mountains. After he purchased the property that later became William S. Hart Park, he reburied Mack here (as seen at the top of the photograph). Although Hart favored purebreds, the grave for "Red" in the picture was short for Newhall Red, a stray mutt that wandered up to Hart's property and lived out the remainder of his days with the dog-loving former movie star.

Three

The Park

HART PARK GATE. The entrance to William S. Hart Park is at the southern end of Old Town Newhall, a dining and entertainment district of Santa Clarita. Newhall's famous Walk of Western Stars begins just outside the park's gates. (Courtesy of Roger and Becki Basham.)

Hart Hall. When visitors enter through the main gates at Hart Park, they are greeted by Hart Hall. In the late 1980s, a pole barn was erected here with uprights supporting a lightweight shingled roof. After the 1994 Northridge earthquake, FEMA converted the structure into a disaster office where earthquake victims could file their claims. The current building was constructed in 1999. It has a large general-purpose meeting room, multiple restrooms, and a full kitchen. It has proven popular as a location for meetings, weddings, concerts, dances, and other events. Behind the hall is a gazebo and a large patio, which opens to a grassy area where a white picket fence surrounds the grave of Fritz, Hart's prized pony. (Courtesy of Jason Lubas.)

Fritz's Grave and Lisbeth Trail. Fritz's grave is one of the must-see locations in William S. Hart Park, but like so many features here, it can easily be missed. Fritz's large stone and bronze memorial can be reached a short distance down a walkway behind Hart Hall. Pictured below is author Kim Stephens posing next to a sign marking three of the many hiking trails in the park. Fritz Road is of course named after Hart's beloved pony who would refuse to work if his mule pal Lisbeth was not nearby. To lessen the tension on set, Hart would let the two animals be together as much as possible. In honor of Lisbeth, another of the hiking trails behind the mansion is named for her. So even though Hart and his equine friend have passed on, Fritz and Lisbeth will forever "meet" behind Hart's home in William S. Hart Park. (Right, courtesy of Ken Lubas; below, E.J. Stephens.)

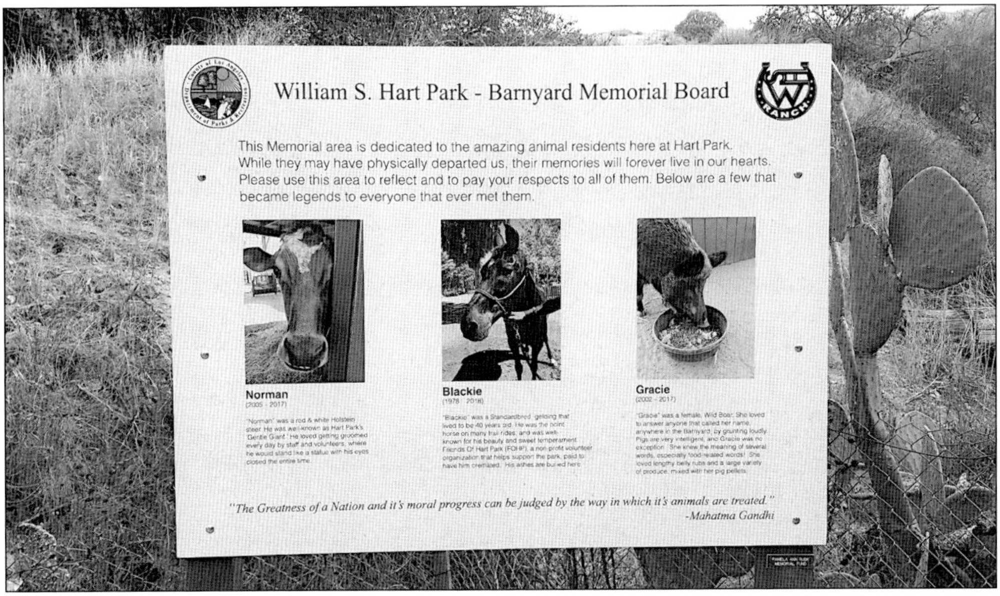

Barnyard Memorial Board. Two of Fritz's four-legged companions—Lisbeth the Mule and studio horse Cactus Kate—are also buried near Fritz. There is also a memorial near the grave dedicated to some of the park's other late great animal friends. Currently, three of them are honored on the memorial. These are the red and white Holstein steer Norman (2005–2017); Blackie, a 40-year-old Standardbred gelding (1978–2018); and Gracie, a female wild boar (2002–2017). The graveyard is at the base of a hill behind Hart Hall. (Both, E.J. Stephens.)

Ranch House. The ranch house was built around 1910 as the residence of George Babcock Smith, the original ranch owner. The building was made of board and batten construction, which allowed for easy exterior wall removal for filming after Hart bought the property. In 1922, Hart remodeled the building with frame and stucco walls and added several more rooms. Bill and Mary Ellen spent much of their time living in the ranch house after Hart's 1925 retirement while their mansion was being built on top of the hill. The ranch house is open several days each week for self-guided tours. Visitors will find many of Hart's possessions inside, including house furnishings, acting props, and his saddles and tack. Notice the Horseshoe Ranch brand crafted from Hart's initials. (Courtesy of Roger and Becki Basham.)

Ranch House II. This bedroom in the ranch house may have been Mary Ellen's room. A couple of things to look for when visiting the ranch house are the old-style (and frankly frightening) original electrical system that ran through the house, and a period dime cemented into the fireplace hearth. Be sure and watch for a Hart movie playing in the living room.

Ranch House III. This alternate view of the ranch house gives a good impression of its size. While the main mansion is filled with artwork and personal belongings, this humbler abode is chock-full of movie props and other interesting items from the early days of Horseshoe Ranch. Be sure and look for "Clyde," the buffalo head that for many years graced the main building's living room until he got a little long in the tooth.

Trading Post. In 2006, a 30-foot modular trailer with a split log exterior was positioned next to the barnyard. A front porch, stone chimney, skirting, and signs were added to the outside while display cases, shelving, rustic wood molding, and curtains were added inside. Every effort was made to have the new store resemble a southwestern trading post, and today shoppers can find a nice variety of authentic Southwestern items, including Native American wares, Western-themed books, first-edition William S. Hart–authored books, movies, music, and home decorations. FOHP operates the nonprofit store to help defray the costs of the barnyard animals and other park programs. (Both, courtesy of Roger and Becki Basham.)

Log Cabin. The original log cabin was built between 1911 and 1918 and was thought to have been a playhouse for the owner's daughter. In 1926, it became the residence for the ranch foreman when the bunkhouse burned down and was used for this purpose for the next several decades. In 1957, it was attached to a second log cabin to create an office when the park opened to the public. In the late 1980s, the older log cabin was turned into a small gift store. When a new gift store was moved onto the ranch, the log cabin was turned into a used bookstore to supplement FOHP programs. (Courtesy of Jason Lubas.)

Frew House. Adjacent to the parking lot for Hart Hall is a parcel of land that formerly belonged to Newhall blacksmith Tom Frew. Frew's 1926 frame and stucco house, a similar outbuilding, and a wood barn were all purchased by the County of Los Angeles in 1958. The main house now serves as the park office. The nearby Heritage Junction structures are on land formerly owned by the Frew family. (E.J. Stephens.)

Four

HERITAGE JUNCTION

THE SANTA CLARITA VALLEY HISTORICAL SOCIETY. The SCVHS was formed in 1975. In 1980, the organization was able to save the Saugus Train Station by moving the structure to Heritage Junction from its location two miles to the north. The beautiful and historic building now serves as the organization's headquarters.

PARDEE HOUSE. Built in 1890 as a Good Templars hall, this house, which sits at the entrance of Heritage Junction, was the former home of Ed Pardee and was located at what is today Veterans Plaza opposite Hart Park (below). The property was sold in 1946 to the Pacific Telephone Company. In 1992, the company donated the building to the SCVHS, and it was moved to Heritage Junction. Plans are underway to convert this structure into a museum of local history. (Left, courtesy of Ken Lubas; below, courtesy of scvhistory.com.)

Newhall Ranch House. This large two-story ranch house was built in 1893 on land now being used for the Magic Mountain amusement park. The structure served as the headquarters for Newhall Ranch, and the ranch foreman lived here until 1973. In 1990, the Newhall Land and Farming Company donated the structure to the SCVHS, and it was moved to Heritage Junction. The image above shows the house at its new location. Below is the house at its old home. (Above, courtesy of scvhistory.com; below, courtesy of Ken Lubas.)

MITCHELL ADOBE. One of the oldest structures in the Santa Clarita Valley was the Mitchell adobe home, which was built in Sand Canyon in 1860. The Mitchell home was occupied for about 20 years before being abandoned, leaving the adobe structure to deteriorate. In 1989, when new developments threatened the adobe, members of the SCVHS gathered a sufficient number of the remaining blocks to build this small structure, which sits opposite the Saugus Train Station in Heritage Junction. (Courtesy of Jessica Boyer.)

SAUGUS TRAIN STATION. The most impressive building at Heritage Park is undoubtedly the Saugus Train Station. It was built in 1887 by the Southern Pacific Railroad two miles north of its current location and served a railroad spur line that went from Saugus to Ventura. The two-story structure housed the station agent and his family upstairs. After the station closed in 1978, the building was saved from destruction by a valiant community program spearheaded by the SCVHS along with Ruth and Scott Newhall, the owners of the *Signal* newspaper. (Courtesy of Ken Lubas.)

Saugus Train Station II. Ruth and Scott Newhall, the owners of the *Signal*, publicized the fundraising efforts needed to move the train station by parking their pickup truck along Railroad Avenue, indicating how far the station could be moved with the money collected at that point. As more money came in, the truck was moved farther down the road. In 1980, they had raised enough funds to move the building in two pieces to its new home at Heritage Junction. Above is a photograph from 1910 showing the train station at its original site on the southeast corner of Railroad Avenue and Drayton Street. Below, the station is being moved to Heritage Junction in 1980.

Charlie Chaplin and Douglas Fairbanks. The train station has served as a local museum and headquarters for the SCVHS for the past four decades. While still at its original location, the station doubled as a filming site for Charlie Chaplin, Frank Sinatra, and others. At left is a still from Chaplin's 1923 movie *The Pilgrim*, which was partially filmed at the station. This image is now on the "Chaplin Door" inside the station. The station is briefly featured in *Wild and Woolly* (1917), which starred Chaplin's best friend, Douglas Fairbanks. In 2020, Tracey Goessel, the author of *The First King of Hollywood: The Life of Douglas Fairbanks*, presented a lecture on Fairbanks at Hart Hall. (Left, E.J. Stephens; below, courtesy of Tracey Goessel.)

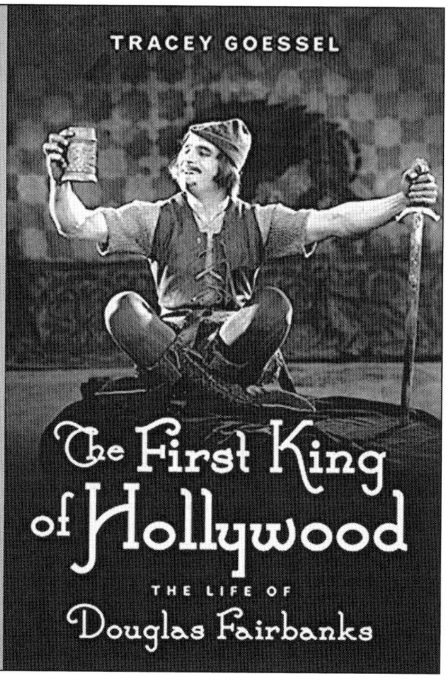

Stars at the Station. The Saugus Train Station was the intended site of a presidential assassination in the 1954 Frank Sinatra film *Suddenly*. In addition to "Old Blue Eyes," the train station has been used as a backdrop for such stars as Douglas Fairbanks, Al Jolson, Charlie Chaplin, and John Wayne. John Cusack appeared in a scene at the station in the 1990 crime drama *The Grifters*.

Mogul Engine No. 1629. In 1981, singing cowboy movie star Gene Autry donated his locomotive, the standard-gauge 2-6-0 Southern Pacific Mogul Engine No. 1629, to the SCVHS. The train had been a part of Autry's Melody Ranch Movie Studio in Newhall for many years and had appeared in countless films and television programs. The historical society had just rescued and moved the Saugus Train Station to Heritage Junction in William S. Hart Park a year earlier. Above is the train at its previous location at Melody Ranch. Below, the train now rests at its current home next to the train station in Heritage Junction. (Above, courtesy of scvhistory.com; below, courtesy of Ken Lubas.)

EDISON HOUSE. A few steps past the Saugus Train Station is an area of preserved historical structures known as Quester Court. The closest home to the entrance of the park is the Edison House, one of several cottages/kit houses built in the 1920s for employees of the Saugus substation of the Southern California Edison Company. The homes were located on what is today Magic Mountain Parkway near Interstate 5. Some of them were destroyed in the St. Francis Dam disaster in 1928. A few were rebuilt, and employees continued to live in the small settlement until 1972, when the company decided to sell the property. The new owner, Newhall Land and Farming Company, allowed all but one of the structures to be destroyed in a fire department exercise. The remaining cottage was moved to Heritage Junction in 1989 and has been repaired and renovated by the SCVHS and the local Quester organizations.

Edison House Interior. The interior of the Edison House has been decorated by Questers with period furniture and appliances, like those seen here in the laundry room. Below is a photograph of the beautifully decorated living room. Tours of the house can be scheduled through the SCVHS. (Both, courtesy of Roger and Becki Basham.)

KINGSBURRY HOUSE. The Kingsburry House was built in 1878 and was originally located on today's Lyons Avenue in Newhall. The property was purchased in 1883 by Lyman Stewart, who was one of the founders of the Union Oil Company. The structure was moved to Walnut Street in 1911. In the 1940s, it was purchased by Charles Kingsburry. In 1987, Jim Droz and Alan Fine acquired the property and donated the home to the SCVHS, which moved it to Heritage Junction. Since its arrival, the structure has been renovated by the SCVHS and local Quester organizations. Like the train station, the Kingsburry House has also appeared on the big screen, seen briefly in the 1982 horror film *Friday the 13th, Part III.* (Courtesy of Roger and Becki Basham.)

Kingsburry House Interior. A wide porch protects the front of the Kingsburry house and offers a cool place to sit on hot summer days. The front door opens to the small living room with an upright piano. A large dining room leads to a kitchen with a wood-burning stove and oven, icebox, and Hoosier cabinet. Two bedrooms and a small bathroom complete this elegant home. (Both, courtesy of Roger and Becki Basham.)

Little Red Schoolhouse. The small portable wood schoolhouse next to the Kingsburry house is typical of those found in frontier communities throughout the West. Its small size only allowed space for a teacher and eight to ten students. This structure was purchased by Robert Callahan in the 1920s and eventually wound up at Callahan's Old West Trading Post on Sierra Highway in Canyon Country. After Callahan's death, his widow donated several of the buildings from the tourist attraction to the SCVHS to be displayed at Heritage Junction.

Ramona Chapel. Author Helen Hunt Jackson wrote the novel *Ramona* in 1884, intending the story to serve as an "*Uncle Tom's Cabin* for Indians," illustrating the sad plight of the Mission Indians of California. The underlying message was missed by most of the reading public, who were more interested in the tragic story of Ramona and her Native American lover Alessandro. Jackson had visited Rancho Camulos in nearby Piru in 1882 while doing research for the novel. Rancho Camulos became a major tourist attraction due to the book's explosive popularity, and people all over the country became obsessed with seeing where the fictional character Ramona once "lived." The Ramona Chapel is a replica of the one that still stands at Rancho Camulos. (Courtesy of Jessica Boyer.)

CAMPGROUND. The tiny Ramona Chapel was built in 1926 by Robert Callahan as a model of the historic chapel at Rancho Camulos in Piru. This building, along with the tiny schoolhouse, was donated in 1987 by Callahan's widow to the SCVHS. To the left is a photograph from 1927 showing the inside of the chapel. Another often overlooked gem found in the park is the campground near Quester Court (below). (Left, courtesy of the *Signal*; below, courtesy of scvhistory.com.)

Five

The Animals

Bison. As hard as it may be to believe, there is actually a herd of bison in downtown Santa Clarita. These beautiful animals, often mistakenly called buffalo, were originally donated to the William S. Hart Park by Walt Disney in the 1960s.

Half Pint. Author Bill West poses with the park's popular donkey Half Pint. Both have appeared in Santa Clarita's Fourth of July parades for the FOHP. Male donkeys are called jacks, and females are known as jennys. If a male donkey and a female horse mate, the offspring is a mule, like Hart's pal Lisbeth. If a male horse and a female donkey mate, the result is a hinny. Donkeys are thought to be stubborn, but in truth, they just have a higher sense of self-preservation and are actually stronger than horses of the same size. In this photograph, Half Pint reminds Bill who is boss with a friendly shirt-nibble. (Courtesy of friendsofhartpark.org.)

Merry the Bison. It is feeding time for Merry the baby bison. No, her name is not a misprint; she was born during the holidays. Sadly, Merry died from malignant catarrhal fever, a disease transmitted from goats and sheep that can kill American bison. Because of the loss of Merry, and out of caution for the rest of the bison herd, it was decided to move the goats and sheep out of the park. (Courtesy of Roger and Becki Basham.)

Huell and Half Pint. In the background above, donkey Half Pint is being interviewed by the late, beloved California historian and television host Huell Howser. In 2007, Howser visited the park to film episode No. 153 of *California's Golden Parks*, one of his many programs about the hidden gems of California. Many of the park's volunteers provided on- and off-camera support to the show. A DVD featuring the episode is available for purchase at the Trading Post gift store. Below, Howser poses with park volunteer extraordinaire Becki Basham. (Both, courtesy of Roger and Becki Basham.)

Rico and Newt. Rico and Newt, the park's pot-bellied pigs, are seen dining on pumpkins donated just after Halloween. Pot-bellied pigs have a belly that curves to the ground, giving them their name. They can be black, white, spotted, or silver, and may even have tusks. They are said to be smarter than cats or dogs. Winston Churchill apparently believed this, as he was quoted as saying, "Dogs look up to you, cats look down on you, and pigs are willing to treat you as an equal." Pictured below are two young ladies greeting Rico. Pot-bellied pigs originally came from Vietnam and were introduced to the United States in 1988. They have become popular pets due to their small size and pleasant dispositions. This is certainly true of Rico, who quickly made friends with his two young visitors. (Both, courtesy of Roger and Becki Basham.)

MONTY. Pictured here is 33-year-old (at the time of writing) quarter horse Monty, a favorite at the park who can often be seen keeping company with donkey Half Pint. Quarter horses are so named because over a short distance (like the quarter-mile), they can outrun most other breeds. Monty might be a little too laid back to demonstrate. Here, he shows his opinion on the park being shut down due to the COVID-19 pandemic. The authors hope that future visitors will see him without his tongue sticking out. (Courtesy of friendsofhartpark.org.)

Norman. Pictured here is beloved red and white Holstein steer Norman. Norman was truly the park's mascot and has been sorely missed since his passing in 2017. Norman was a gentle giant who will always be remembered for his engaging, toothy smile and sweet nature. When Norman was still alive, he had a benign tumor in his stomach, which made him look pregnant. Very often, volunteers had to explain to guests that pregnancy is not an option for steers. Today, there is a sign by his former pen commemorating Norman's years of outstanding guest relations in the park. (Courtesy of Ken Lubas.)

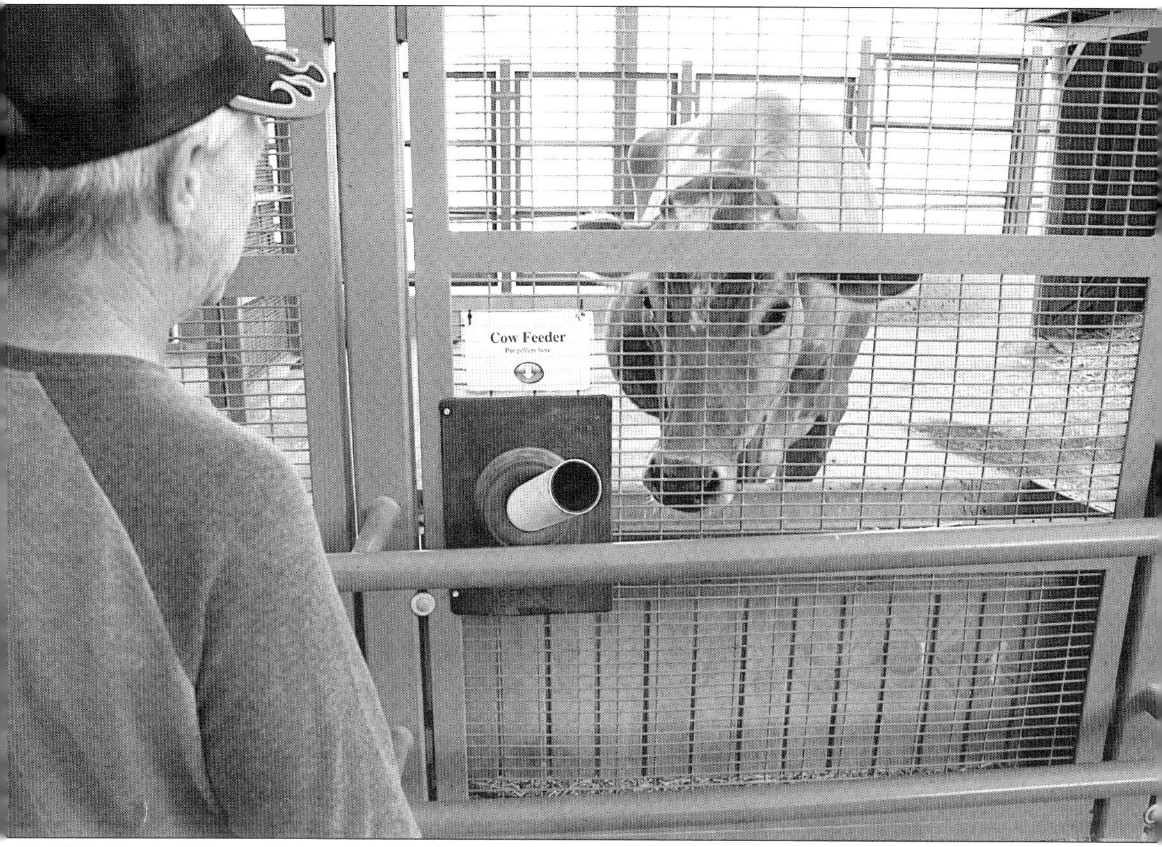

Cow Feeder. Generally, steers go to slaughter since they are castrated bulls not used for breeding. Holsteins are known for their large size and prominent hipbones. Norman originally came to Hart Park from a family that had gotten him to raise and ultimately slaughter for food. However, Norman charmed them—like he did all who met him—and they did not have the heart to go through with it. So, in July 2009, Norman was donated to the park, where he lived until 2017—a very long life for a steer. Guests loved feeding him, but the feed often went into his nose, so a "cow feeder" tube (seen here) was installed to allow guests to safely feed their favorite bovine. The new stars of the park, the alpacas, now reside in Norman's old pen. (Courtesy Ken Lubas.)

Irwin. Late emu Irwin is pictured here. Emus are the second largest bird in the world after ostriches, and have two sets of eyelids, one for blinking and the other for protecting their eyes from dust. Originally from Australia, an emu's wings will not allow them to fly but do help them keep cool. They also help emus keep their balance when they sprint at up to 30 miles per hour. (Courtesy of friendsofhartpark.org.)

Leia and Luke. There are not only pot-bellied pigs at Hart Park, but also wild boars. Pictured here is Leia the boar along with former staff member Stefani Perez. (Luke the boar is out of the frame. Their names are a wink to *Star Wars* fans.) Unlike pot-bellied pigs, wild boars can weigh half a ton and therefore do not make good house pets. (Courtesy of Ray Kimura.)

Sylvia, Rachael, and Alpacas. Barnyard volunteer Sylvia Altamirano is pictured at right with alpacas Clarisse and Chanel. Sylvia was the recipient of the inaugural Hart Park Volunteer of the Month award. Below, park animal keeper Rachael Komulainen is the greatest friend of the park's animals. Her enthusiasm is boundless, and all the humans and animals at the park owe her a debt of gratitude. She is pictured here with some of the park's alpacas. Each has a name that begins with the letter "C." In this photograph are Cruella, Carma, Clarice, Coco, and Chanel.

Bill and Mary Ellen. Hart Park is the home of a pair of Sulcata tortoises named Bill and Mary Ellen. Sulcatas are one of the largest tortoises in the world and can reach the size of tractor tires. They can also live 150 years. Bill and Mary Ellen are still in their 20s, which means they are babies in the tortoise world and will help keep the memory of their namesakes alive for at least another century. Above, Jessica Boyer interviews the park's animal keepers for local television station SCVTV. Below, author Bill West holds Mary Ellen alongside son Josh and wife Liliana. (Above, courtesy of scvnews.com; below, courtesy of friendsofhartpark.org.)

Feeding the Animals. Some of the animals at Hart Park can be fed by the visitors, like the chickens seen in the photograph to the right. Feed for the animals is available for purchase at the Trading Post gift store. The staff in the gift shop can answer questions about these feathered and furry friends. William S. Hart Park animal keeper Rachael Komulainen is shown below with popular donkey pal Half Pint. (Right, courtesy of Ken Lubas; below, courtesy of scvnews.com.)

WATERFOWL HABITAT. This view of the waterfowl habitat (also known as "the duck pond") shows a lovely enclosure, but further improvements are happening in the area as this book goes to press. The staff is thrilled to report that the finishing touches are being applied to a new, improved waterfowl habitat that includes a custom cover that will allow the park's fowl to enjoy the pond at all hours of the day and night. Previously, they were marched into an enclosure every evening to keep them safe from predators. (Courtesy of scvnews.com.)

Deer Abby. Another park favorite is Deer Abby (get it?). Abby is being greeted here by two youngsters. She is often missed by visitors to the park because she lives in a pen up on the hillside. Today, Abby lives with her mule deer friend Willow. Often overlooked by guests busy checking out the pigs, bison, and alpacas is a flock of fowl, including ducks, swans, and chickens. Some other spots that are easy to miss include the final resting place of Hart's pony Fritz, the dogs' graveyard, the hiking trails, the campground, the bunkhouse, and the bison viewing area outside the park just off Market Street. Park staff or volunteers will gladly direct visitors to these hidden gems. (Above, courtesy of scvnews.com; below, Kim Stephens.)

Bison II. Legend has it that shortly after Walt Disney imported a small herd of American bison to his Golden Oak movie ranch in Newhall, the creatures got a bit ornery and chased Disney's brother Roy onto the roof of a car. At that point, Walt's wife, Lillian, demanded their removal and the herd was quickly donated to William S. Hart Park. It is thrilling to be at Hart Park during feeding time when the dinner bell rings and these majestic creatures come out to eat. The bison fit in beautifully with their surroundings, and Hart himself would be proud to know these great "American buffalo" are roaming his land. Guests can view the bison in Hart Park on the way up to the mansion. (Courtesy of Roger and Becki Basham.)

Six

The People

Pictured here are many of the staff members who make William S. Hart Park such a wonderful place. These folks, along with all the amazing volunteers, are the true lifeblood of the park. Numerous volunteer opportunities are available throughout the park. (Courtesy of Roger and Becki Basham.)

JACK, MARGI, AND JOANNE. Jack Stewart is a true Old West history buff who has appeared in several Western films. He is also one of the beloved volunteers of FOHP, serving on the board of directors. Below, Margi Bertram (left) is the recently retired—but still very much involved—administrator of Hart's mansion. She is pictured here with Joanne Grosh, one of the park's most dedicated volunteers. Grosh was being honored by the County of Los Angeles for 35 continuous years of volunteer service.

Ayla, Laurene, Rachael, and Alan. Even a global pandemic cannot keep the operations of William S. Hart Park down. Although the staff was cut back due to COVID-19, the alpacas still got to go on a walk with, from left to right, volunteer Ayla Mouchawar, FOHP president Laurene Weste, and animal keeper Rachael Komulainen. At right, Alan Pollack has an impressive day job; he is a medical doctor, but in the spare time he can muster, he also happens to be the president of the SCVHS, which is headquartered in the Heritage Junction section of William S. Hart Park. Pollack began his rise to the historical society presidency as a volunteer docent.

Duane Harte. Pictured here is the late Duane Harte with his wife, Pauline. He was a Santa Clarita Valley resident and super volunteer who, for many years, was the treasurer of the SCVHS. But his volunteering activities did not end there. Harte served with organizations such as Friends of Mentryville, the Santa Clarita Valley (SCV) Chamber of Commerce, the SCV Committee on Aging, the SCV Senior Center Charitable Foundation, the Newhall Redevelopment Committee, the SCV Historical Veterans Plaza Committee, Friends of the Libraries of the SCV, the Canyon Theatre Guild, Zonta, the Elks lodge, and the American Legion. Harte passed away suddenly in 2015 and is greatly missed. Someone as dedicated to the community as him should have a park named after him, which is exactly what happened in 2016.

HUELL, ROGER, AND GUY. Volunteer Roger Basham (right) is pictured above with Huell Howser during the filming of an episode of Howser's television series *California's Golden Parks* featuring William S. Hart Park. Basham tries to stay in the background, supporting his wife, Becki, in maintaining the Trading Post gift store. But his efforts are too substantial to stay hidden for long. Basham added a bookstore to the park, which is open during special events. He also provided many of the photographs used in this book, along with a ton of research that the authors very much appreciate. Below is volunteer Guy Horanburg working on Mogul Engine No. 1629, a locomotive that was donated to the Santa Clarita Valley Historical Society in 1981 by none other than singing cowboy star Gene Autry.

PAM, JEFF, AND NIKKI. Jeff Wheat, another of the board of directors of the FOHP, is shown above with his wife, Pam, who both work in "the biz." In his day job, Jeff is an Emmy Award–winning cameraman, and for the FOHP, he brings a sense of duty and detail to everything he puts his hand to, often working long hours behind the scenes. Volunteer Nikki Smith is shown at left with Monty, a popular 30-something quarter horse. (Both, courtesy of friendsofhartpark.org.)

Becki, Bill, Tom, and Tim. At right are park volunteers Becki Basham and Bill Crowl. The book they are holding is William S. Hart's 1929 autobiography, *My Life: East and West*. By 2000, it had been long out of print, and Crowl, Basham, and her husband, Roger, made it their mission to see it back in print. Thanks to their tireless efforts, Hart's autobiography is again available at the park's Trading Post gift store, which Becki manages. Below, the FOHP makes wise use of its volunteers' natural talents. On the left is Tom Hough, a CPA by day, who is the treasurer of the FOHP in his off-hours. On the right is Tim Murphy, an FOHP board member who happens to be an artist. The poster they hold is a "Fun Map," which Murphy created to help visitors find their way around the park. (Right, courtesy of Roger and Becki Basham; below, courtesy of friendsofhartpark.org.)

SCVHS. Heritage Junction is the home of the SCVHS. A recent gathering of the board of directors inside the Saugus Train Station is pictured above. This group sponsors historical tours throughout the year, like the one in late March to the nearby site of the St. Francis Dam disaster, where hundreds of people were killed in 1928. Shown below from left to right are Alan Pollack, president of the SCVHS, and fellow board members Dianne Hellrigel, Laurene Weste, and Ann Stansell. Pollack and Hellrigel shepherded the Saint Francis Dam Disaster National Memorial and National Monument Act through Congress in 2019.

Al and Bob. Al Ewing (left) and Bob Hill are seen here helping out at the park's annual holiday boutique in Hart Hall. Ewing served for many years as an event coordinator at the park before his recent retirement. Hill, who passed away in 2021, was the soft-spoken, kind-hearted president of the FOHP volunteers for five years. (Courtesy of Roger and Becki Basham.)

Brandon and Eric. Los Angeles County employee Brandon Matthews (left) and park superintendent Eric Reifman are being led around by two of the park's popular alpacas, Carma and Cruella. (Courtesy of Roger and Becki Basham.)

Leon Worden. One of the premier local historians of the Santa Clarita Valley, Leon Worden is also a former president of the SCVHS. Worden is a well-known local media personality and former writer and editor of the *Signal* newspaper. He currently runs SCVTV and internet news and information outlets SCVTV.com and scvhistory.com. Many of the photographs and information in this book came from these sources. When not writing articles or attending one of his many board of director meetings, Worden can be found working on the restoration of Mogul Engine No. 1629, the locomotive that sits beside the Saugus Train Station.

Seven

THE EVENTS

TRAIN STATION EVENT. William S. Hart Park is replete with varied locations, including acres of lawn, picnic grounds, a meeting hall, a gazebo, a mansion, and several historic buildings. The range of events that can be held here is as varied as the locations. Seen here is a group of young dancers celebrating Hispanic culture at the Saugus Train Station.

Cowboy Festival. Every spring, the City of Santa Clarita hosts the Santa Clarita Cowboy Festival in William S. Hart Park and Old Town Newhall. Thousands of fans of Old Western cuisine and culture come together for a weekend in April to enjoy Old West food, dancing, and musical performances, often clad in Western duds. Many popular Western performers, like Don Edwards, regularly appear at the festival. (Both, courtesy of Roger and Becki Basham.)

Line Dances and Book Sales. Above is a country line-dancing class that was presented by FOHP board member Nancy Gallardo. Below is a look at one of the many book sales that take place in the park during special events. In this photograph is favorite bookworm Roger Basham setting up for a sale at a recent Hart of the West Pow Wow. (Both, courtesy of Roger and Becki Basham.)

Cowboy Festival and Car Show. In addition to the aforementioned events, Cowboy Festival guests can also hear cowboy poetry, sample Dutch oven peach cobbler and chili at the cowboy cook-off, practice panning for gold, or try their skills at archery, or even hatchet throwing! The Cowboy Festival has so many events that even the spacious William S. Hart Park cannot contain them all. Some performances are held in venues around Old Town Newhall (above). One-time events, as opposed to annual ones, often pop up in the park, like the car show seen below in 2018. (Both, courtesy of Roger and Becki Basham.)

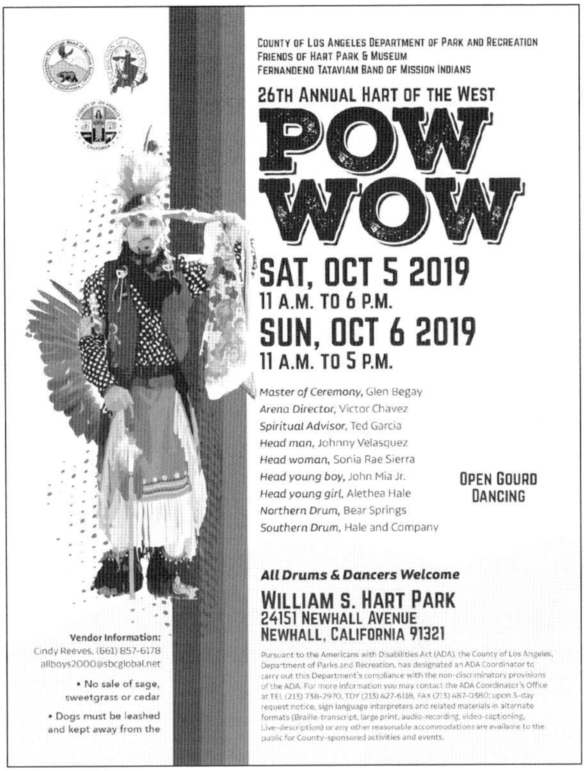

Pow Wow. The Santa Clarita Cowboy Festival is not the only large annual festival hosted at the park. Every year, Native Americans gather for the Hart of the West Pow Wow. This gathering is sponsored by both the Los Angeles County Department of Parks and Recreation and the Fernandeno Tataviam Band of Mission Indians.

Silents Under the Stars. Hart Park hosts several annual festivals, including the Santa Clarita Cowboy Festival, Bow Wows & Meows, Hart of the West Pow Wow, the Santa Clarita Polynesian Festival, the Newhallywood Silent Film Festival, and Cowboys and Carols. Pictured here is one of the most popular annual events, Silents Under the Stars, which features an outdoor dinner and the presentation of a William S. Hart film with live accompaniment. At left is legendary late performer Johnny Crawford, who played Mark McCain on television's *The Rifleman*, visiting with FOHP president and Santa Clarita councilwoman Laurene Weste at a recent Silents Under the Stars event. (Both, courtesy of Roger and Becki Basham.)

Music, Music, Music! Music is a constant at William S. Hart Park. Whether it is a concert in Hart Hall, a musical being shown on an outdoor screen, a wedding procession, or a dance, the sounds of Hart Park enchant visitors throughout the year. Above, a singer/guitarist performs at a recent Santa Clarita Cowboy Festival. Below, the Grateful Dudes entertain a Silents Under the Stars crowd. (Both, courtesy of Roger and Becki Basham.)

Clubs. William S. Hart Park's Hart Hall is often the choice for clubs to hold their events, like the Wild West Rose Show, an annual event held by the Santa Clarita Rose Society. Every fall, Hart Hall becomes a model train aficionado's paradise, as the High Desert Modular Railroad Club takes over the hall, to the delight of kids of all ages.

Holiday Gatherings. In addition to all of the usual holiday events, December 6 is William S. Hart's birthday, and the staff cannot let that day pass without a party—Cowboys and Carols. In 2013, Hart's birthday was celebrated with cowboy balladeer Don Edwards performing in Hart's living room. Also serenading guests in the foyer that evening was the violinist seen at right. (Both, courtesy of Roger and Becki Basham.)

SILENT FILM. Because of its ties to one of the biggest silent film stars, William S. Hart Park has become a gathering spot for Southern California fans of silent film. At left, the annual Newhallywood Silent Film Festival takes place at the park every year in February. Below, a slapstick and melodrama workshop was held inside Hart's mansion during the 2020 festival. (Left, courtesy of newhallywoodfilmfest.org; below, courtesy of friendsofhartpark.org.)

Leonard Maltin and Tippi Hedren. In 2011, renowned movie critic Leonard Maltin and silver screen legend Tippi Hedren came to Heritage Junction to help honor the 75th anniversary of the release of the Charlie Chaplin classic *Modern Times*, which was partly filmed nearby. Below, Tippi poses at the park with a stand-up of Chaplin. Hedren appeared in Chaplin's final film, *A Countess from Hong Kong* (1967). (Both, E.J. Stephens.)

CHAPLINFEST. At left, Leonard Maltin and Tippi Hedren recreate the Charlie Chaplin–Paulette Goddard walk from the final scene of *Modern Times*—one of the most famous scenes in film history—on Sierra Highway near Agua Dulce, just a short drive from Hart Park. As part of the ChaplinFest celebration in 2011, the black granite monument below was donated to Heritage Junction. Plans are in motion to place the monument at the filming site. (Both, E.J. Stephens.)

About the Organizations

Our Partners. The operation of William S. Hart Park requires dozens of dedicated people from several different organizations. The land, animals, and buildings are managed by the Los Angeles County Department of Parks and Recreation. The items inside Hart's mansion are managed by the Natural History Museum of Los Angeles County. William S. Hart Park also serves as the headquarters of two volunteer organizations: the Friends of Hart Park and Museum, which helps maintain and promote the park, and the Santa Clarita Valley Historical Society, which promotes historic preservation. All these groups rely on one major resource: their volunteers. To learn more about making donations or volunteering, please visit the websites below. (E.J. Stephens.)

Los Angeles County Department of Parks and Recreation	www.parks.lacounty.gov
Natural History Museum of Los Angeles County	www.nhm.org
Friends of Hart Park and Museum	www.friendsofhartpark.org
Santa Clarita Valley Historical Society	www.scvhs.org